FULLY DEVOTED

From FIRST STEPS *to*
FULLY SURRENDERED

Lifeway Press®
Brentwood, Tennessee

EDITORIAL TEAM

Cynthia Hopkins
Writer

Tyler Quillet
Managing Editor

Reid Patton
Senior Editor

Joel Polk
Publisher, Small Group Publishing

Katie Vogel
Assistant Editor

John Paul Basham
Director, Adult Ministry Publishing

Jon Rodda
Art Director

Published by Lifeway Press® • © 2024 Kendrick Bros., LLC

ISBN 978-1-4300-9388-6 • Item 005847376

Dewey decimal classification: 248.84

Subject headings: CHRISTIAN LIFE \ DISCIPLESHIP \ JESUS CHRIST—LORDSHIP

To order additional copies of this resource, write to Lifeway Resources Customer Service; 200 Powell Place, Suite 100; Brentwood, TN 37027-7707; fax 615-251-5933; call toll free 800-458-2772; order online at Lifeway.com; or email orderentry@lifeway.com.

Printed in the United States of America

Adult Ministry Publishing • Lifeway Resources • 200 Powell Place, Suite 100 • Brentwood, TN 37027-7707

CONTENTS

ABOUT THE AUTHORS

STEPHEN KENDRICK is a writer, speaker, and film producer with a passion for sharing the truth and love of Jesus among the nations. He produces the Kendrick Brothers' films and has cowritten (with Alex) the *New York Times* bestsellers *The Love Dare*, *The Resolution for Men*, and *The Battle Plan for Prayer*. Stephen is a frequent speaker on marriage, fatherhood, discipleship, and prayer. He and his wife, Jill, have six children.

ALEX KENDRICK is an accomplished author, actor, and film director, whose credits include *Facing the Giants, Fireproof, Courageous, War Room, Overcomer*, and, most recently, *The Forge*. A creative artist with a pastor's heart, Alex speaks internationally on the power of film and the surpassing power of Christ. He and his wife, Christina, have six children.

FULLY DEVOTED

HOW TO USE THIS STUDY

This Bible study book includes eight weeks of content for group and personal study.

GROUP SESSIONS

Regardless of what day of the week your group meets, each week of content begins with the group session. These sessions are meant to facilitate simple yet meaningful interaction among group members through God's Word and the teaching of Priscilla Shirer and Stephen and Alex Kendrick. Each group session uses the following format.

START. This page includes questions to get the conversation started and to introduce the video teaching.

WATCH. This page provides space to take notes on the video teaching.

Codes to access the video teaching are included with your purchase of this book and can be found on the insert located at the back of this book.

Slow or unreliable internet connection? Your Bible study videos can be downloaded to your device so you can play them offline. Simply download your videos on the Lifeway OnDemand App when you are in a place with strong internet connection. Then, you'll be able to watch your session videos anywhere, any time. Look for the download symbol beside your video.

DISCUSS. This page includes questions and statements that guide the group to respond to the Kendricks' video teaching and explore relevant Bible passages.

PERSONAL STUDY

Each week includes five days of personal Bible study and learning activities for individual engagement between group sessions. The personal study revisits Scriptures and themes introduced in the video teaching so that participants can understand and apply them on a personal level. The days are numbered 1–5 to provide personal reading and activities for each day of the week, leaving two days off to worship with your church family and to meet as a small group. If your group meets on the same day as your worship gathering, use the extra day to reflect on what God is teaching you and to practice putting the biblical principles into action.

TIPS FOR LEADING A SMALL GROUP

PRAYERFULLY PREPARE

Prepare for each group session with prayer. Ask the Holy Spirit to work through you and the group discussion as you point others to Jesus through God's Word.

REVIEW the personal studies and the group sessions ahead of time.

PRAY for each person in the group.

MINIMIZE DISTRACTIONS

Do everything in your ability to help people focus on what's most important: connecting with God, with the Bible, and with one another.

Create a comfortable environment. If group members are uncomfortable, they'll be distracted and therefore not engage in the group experience.

Take into consideration seating, temperature, lighting, refreshments, surrounding noise, and general cleanliness.

Thoughtfulness and hospitality show guests and group members they're welcome and valued in whatever environment you choose to gather. And even if your guests don't fully recognize your effort, taking these steps will ensure that they will not be distracted during your group discussion.

INCLUDE OTHERS

Your goal is to foster a community in which people are welcome just as they are but encouraged to grow spiritually. Always be aware of opportunities to include anyone who visits the group and invite new people to join your group.

ENCOURAGE DISCUSSION

A good small-group experience has the following characteristics.

EVERYONE PARTICIPATES. Encourage everyone to ask questions, share responses, or read aloud.

NO ONE DOMINATES—NOT EVEN THE LEADER. Be sure your time speaking as a leader takes up less than half of your time together as a group. Politely guide and redirect the discussion if one of the group members dominates.

NOBODY IS RUSHED THROUGH QUESTIONS. Don't feel that a moment of silence is a bad thing. People often need time to think about their responses to questions they've just heard or to work up the courage to share what God is stirring in their hearts.

INPUT IS AFFIRMED AND FOLLOWED UP. Make sure you point out something true or helpful in a response. Don't just move on. Build community with follow-up questions, asking how other people have experienced similar things or how a truth has shaped their understanding of God and the Scripture you're studying. People are less likely to speak up if they fear that you don't actually want to hear their answers or that you're looking for only a certain answer.

GOD AND HIS WORD ARE CENTRAL. Opinions and experiences can be helpful, but God has given us the truth. Trust Scripture to be the authority and God's Spirit to work in people's lives. You can't change anyone, but God can. Continually point people to the Word and to active steps of faith.

KEEP CONNECTING

Think of ways to connect with group members during the week. Participation during the group session always improves when members spend time connecting with one another outside the group sessions. The more people are comfortable with each other and involved in one another's lives, the more they'll look forward to being together. When group members move beyond being friendly to truly being friends who form a community, they come to each session eager to engage instead of merely attending.

ABOUT THE MOVIE

Isaiah Wright has some growing up to do. A year out of high school with no plans for his future, Isaiah is challenged by his single mom and a successful businessman to start charting a better course for his life. Through the prayers of his mother and biblical discipleship from his new mentor, Isaiah begins to discover that God's purpose for his life is so much more than he could hope for or imagine. From the Kendrick Brothers, the creators of the number one hit *War Room*, comes *The Forge*, a faith-filled movie with old friends and inspiring twists.

IN THEATERS AUGUST 2024

FROM THE KENDRICK BROTHERS • CREATORS OF WAR ROOM, OVERCOMER AND COURAGEOUS

CAMERON
ARNETT

PRISCILLA
SHIRER

KAREN
ABERCROMBIE

AND INTRODUCING
ASPEN
KENNEDY

THE FORGE

WHOEVER WANTS THE NEXT GENERATION THE MOST WILL GET THEM

THEFORGEMOVIE.COM AFFIRM FILMS AND FAITHSTEP FILMS PRESENT A PROVIDENT FILMS KENDRICK BROTHERS PRODUCTION "THE FORGE" BEVERLY HOLLOWAY ANNA REDMON ZACK LEEFEW MARCELA SHAW ALEX KENDRICK BILL EBEL BOB M. SCOTT SHARI RIGBY LARRY FRENZEL KEVIN BOUREN SHANNON KENDRICK JIM McBRIDE JUSTIN TOLLEY AARON BURNS TREY REYNOLDS STEPHEN KENDRICK ALEX KENDRICK & STEPHEN KENDRICK ALEX KENDRICK

THEFORGEMOVIE.COM @FORGEMOVIE
EXCLUSIVELY IN THEATERS AUGUST 23

SONY AFFIRM FILMS

FOR INFORMATION ON ADVANCE BUYOUTS AND GROUP SALES, MAKE REQUESTS AT WWW.SONYPICTURESGROUPSALES.COM.
QUESTIONS? EMAIL: GROUPSALES@SONYPICTURES.COM PHONE: 877-488-4258

WEEK 1

COME TO ME

START

Welcome everyone to session 1, "Come to Me."
Ask participants to introduce themselves. As they do, invite them to
share one daring, adventurous thing they have done in their lives.

When you consider the call Jesus gives you to follow Him, does that strike you as a "daring" decision? Explain.

This week's title, "Come to Me," likely strikes different people in different ways. A person who lives with deep regret over personal decisions might think that invitation is only for someone else. A person who has recently decided to follow Jesus might be eagerly anticipating what Jesus's invitation involves. A person who has been a Christian for years might think it has little application in their lives because they answered that invitation long ago.

Jesus's invitation means more than any of us might imagine—and we begin to realize that as we learn His example to us, realize His impact on us, and experience His life in us. The life of a disciple of Jesus Christ is a daring adventure for all of us, whether we are coming to Him in faith for the very first time or we are continuing a journey with Him that started years ago.

With this in mind, what do you hope to gain from this study on what it means to be fully devoted to Jesus?

To prepare for video session 1, pray together.

God, help each of us accept Your invitation to do a daring

thing and decide that we're going to seek You.

WATCH

Use these statements to follow along as you watch video session 1.

Coming to Jesus for salvation is a gift of grace.

EPHESIANS 2:8-9

God takes us deeper and reveals more of Himself as we seek Him.

HEBREWS 11:6

We want to go our own way thinking we don't need God, but He continuously looks for and helps those who are seeking Him.

PSALM 14:2,5-7

DISCUSS

After viewing the video, discuss the following questions with your group.

Read Hebrews 11:6 and Ephesians 2:8-9. What is the starting point for any person to be fully devoted to God? Why?

How do you respond to knowing that God wants to take you deeper in relationship with Him than you are currently?

Alex explained that "God takes us deeper and reveals more of Himself as we seek Him." In what ways has already God done that in your life?

Read Psalm 14. What does this psalm teach you about who you are and who God is?

Stephen challenged us to do a daring thing and choose to seek the Lord. What steps can you take in the days ahead to make that daring choice?

Close in prayer.

Prayer Requests:

DAY 1
THE INVITATION OF JESUS TO YOU

Follow Me. Each of the four Gospel accounts record Jesus repeating those two words multiple times and to various people in different circumstances. It is an open invitation, yet Scripture records no instance where a person's *yes* was accepted by way of compromise. There were those who tried—with what might seem to us to be perfectly good reasons. Still, Jesus never expressed His invitation to come and follow Him as a choice of anything less than total devotion. That's important for us to know! We are tempted to create our own definitions about following Christ. But Jesus defines what it means to come to Him for salvation— we don't. And His invitation completely changes our lives.

Use the chart to record who Jesus invited to follow Him and what accepting that invitation required.

	Who Jesus Invited	What Was Required
Matthew 4:18-20		
Mark 2:14		
Luke 9:59-60		
Matthew 10:1-6,37-39		
Mark 8:34-35		
Mark 10:17-22		
John 1:43		
John 10:24-28		
John 12:20-26		
John 13:36-38		
John 21:18-22		

When did you first hear Jesus's invitation to follow Him? Did you respond with total devotion? How can you respond with total devotion now?

Jesus makes it clear: He's inviting you to something more than intellectual agreement that He is Savior and Lord. He's calling you to abandon everything else and find your security, identity, and purpose in Him. He also makes it clear that if you answer that call, you will gain far more than you could ever possibly lose.

What does Matthew 13:44 teach you about what it's like and what it's worth to follow Jesus?

Following Jesus is like: Following Jesus is worth:

What does Matthew 13:45-46 teach you about what it's like and what it's worth to follow Jesus?

Following Jesus is like: Following Jesus is worth:

Accepting Jesus's invitation changes everything because it demands everything—and offers so much more in return. The price you'll pay to accept Jesus's invitation pales in comparison to the treasure you'll receive in knowing and following Him. His kingdom is worth everything you have and are.

What do you need to do to experience the joy and satisfaction of God's kingdom treasure?

Reflect on the following words from Jesus to you and all His followers. Thank Him for His open invitation to come and follow Him and receive the only treasure that will satisfy your soul.

> *"Come to me, all of you who are weary and burdened, and I will give you rest.*
> *Take my yoke upon you and learn from me, because I am lowly and humble in heart,*
> *and you will find rest for your souls. For my yoke is easy and my burden is light."*
> **MATTHEW 11:28-30**

DAY 2
THE EXAMPLE OF JESUS FOR YOU

Name one reason why it is hard for you to live fully devoted to following Jesus.

Jesus's invitation to follow Him is a big, life-changing ask. When we consider it in light of the earthly treasures we pursue or attain, it can seem impossible. That's the way it hit the rich young ruler in Mark 10:17-22. That guy certainly isn't alone. What's hard for any of us to see on the front end of the decision to follow is that Jesus doesn't leave us on our own to carry it out. He is willing to be fully devoted to us from beginning to end.

> *Now since the children have flesh and blood in common, Jesus also shared in these, so that through his death he might destroy the one holding the power of death—that is, the devil—and free those who were held in slavery all their lives by the fear of death.*
> **HEBREWS 2:14-15**

According to Hebrews, what do you have in common with Jesus?

Why is it important that Jesus knows and has experienced everything you have or ever will experience?

Jesus took on the fullness of your humanity—because He loves you. When He came to earth, He became "flesh and blood" to share in all the emotion and temptation human experience contains. He lived in the world as you do, with one critical difference—He never sinned. Jesus's invitation to come and follow Him is one of complete understanding. He is the ultimate example.

The Word became flesh and dwelt among us. We observed his glory,
the glory as the one and only Son from the Father, full of grace and truth.
JOHN 1:14

They were astonished at his teaching because he was teaching
them as one who had authority, and not like the scribes.
MARK 1:22

In addition to perfect obedience to God's commands, in what other ways is Jesus's life an example to you?

Following Jesus is about more than learning from the greatest teacher of all time (though it is certainly not less than that). Through His flesh-and-blood life, we see God's glory. We learn through Jesus's example and teaching the fullness of grace and the fullness of truth. We can embody these same truths with His divine help.

Jesus is the greatest person who has ever lived. He is the greatest teacher of all time. He is the most loving, selfless person the world has ever known or will ever know. And He took on your humanity perfectly so that you can know and walk alongside Him for all eternity.

Adopt the same attitude as that of Christ Jesus,
who, existing in the form of God,
did not consider equality with God
as something to be exploited.
Instead he emptied himself
by assuming the form of a servant,
taking on the likeness of humanity.
And when he had come as a man,
he humbled himself by becoming obedient
to the point of death—
even to death on a cross.
PHILIPPIANS 2:5-8

Thank Jesus for taking on your humanity so that you can know and follow Him. Ask Him to show you ways you can better follow His example. Fully devote yourself to walking alongside Him in His instruction.

DAY 3
THE IMPACT OF JESUS ON YOU

Jesus Christ has had more impact on the world than anyone else in history. Few argue this fact. Even unbelievers through the centuries have acknowledged the vast influence Jesus has had on music, art, poetry, science, philosophy, human rights, human behavior, and more. His impact is so significant that He became the dividing line of history—B.C. ("before Christ") and A.D. ("anno domini," which means "in the year of our Lord.")

Yet His impact reaches much farther than general historical or cultural influence. If we consider Handel's *Messiah*, Da Vinci's *The Last Supper*, and Dante's *Inferno* as the ultimate examples of Jesus's influence, we've missed the point. Jesus didn't come to make your life better; He came to change it altogether. When you answer Jesus's call to come and follow, His impact on you doesn't end when you take your last breath—it lasts throughout eternity!

Read Jesus's seven "I AM" statements from the Gospel of John. In each verse, circle who Jesus is and underline the resulting impact He has on your life. Then, below each one, write what it means to you personally.

"I am the bread of life," Jesus told them. "No one who comes to me will ever be hungry, and no one who believes in me will ever be thirsty again.
JOHN 6:35

Jesus spoke to them again: "I am the light of the world. Anyone who follows me will never walk in the darkness but will have the light of life."
JOHN 8:12

"I am the gate. If anyone enters by me, he will be saved
and will come in and go out and find pasture."
JOHN 10:9

"I am the good shepherd. The good shepherd lays down his life for the sheep.
JOHN 10:11

Jesus said to her, "I am the resurrection and the life. The
one who believes in me, even if he dies, will live."
JOHN 11:25

Jesus told him, "I am the way, the truth, and the life. No
one comes to the Father except through me."
JOHN 14:6

"I am the vine; you are the branches. The one who remains in me and I in
him produces much fruit, because you can do nothing without me."
JOHN 15:5

Considering these truths about Jesus, what testimony can you give about Jesus's impact on you?

What kind of change do you need to experience in your life? Reflect on what you underlined regarding how who Jesus is impacts you. What do you need to do to experience Jesus in this way?

As you conclude today's study, thank Jesus for His impact on you by praying the seven "I AM" statements. Change each "I am" to "You are," and ask God to help you live in such a way that others see the significance of Jesus's impact on you.

DAY 4
THE LIFE OF JESUS IN YOU

What is one word you would use to describe your life?

> *"A thief comes only to steal and kill and destroy. I have come so that they may have life and have it in abundance."*
> **JOHN 10:10**

Based on this Scripture, what two invitations do we receive every day? What are their effects?

How have you seen the reality of this verse in your life?

Think about everything you've learned this week so far. Answering Jesus's invitation to come and follow Him requires total devotion. It also means you'll find Him to be the only treasure that is worth making such a life-altering decision. And while the path you'll take in following Jesus isn't easy, He doesn't leave you to walk it alone. He has given you His life as an example, His Word as instruction, and His Spirit as your ever-present help. That's not all! While you are becoming more like Jesus, He fills you to complete satisfaction, lights your way in the darkness, and impacts others through you. It's easy to see why Jesus said that life in Him is abundant!

And it is a choice to receive that abundance each day of your life. That doesn't mean you can lose your salvation—you can't. Once you choose to trust and follow Jesus, you are a child of God, always and forever. But walking in the abundant life

He gives is a *daily decision*. As Jesus offers you the invitation to come and follow Him each moment of each day, Satan tempts you to turn away. His aim is death and destruction. Jesus's gift is an eternal abundance of life.

And my God will supply all your needs
according to his riches in glory in Christ Jesus.
PHILIPPIANS. 4:19

Read Philippians 4:10-19. What words or phrases did Paul use that infer the abundant life of Jesus in him?

What is the promise of abundant life in verse 19?

Paul wrote Philippians from a first-century prison cell. His life was not one any of us would look at and consider "abundant." Yet he used that very word to describe himself: fully supplied, in abundance. Even more, he was joyful and content. In his difficult circumstance, Paul experienced the abundant life of Jesus in himself and knew these Philippian believers would, too. And so can you. The abundant life of Jesus in you is a future eternal promise, and it is also a promise for *today*.

Read Matthew 6:25-34. What are some worries that tend to make you think and act as though your life is less abundant than the life Jesus offers?

Read verse 33 again. How can you experience the abundant life of Jesus in you— even in those worries?

Thank Jesus for the abundant life He gives you, now and for eternity. Acknowledge the ways Satan is trying to wreck the abundant joy and contentment of Jesus in you. Ask God to help you to seek His kingdom and righteousness above all else.

DAY 5
NEXT STEPS TO FOLLOW

"One step forward, two steps back." This is a well-known phrase and an even more deeply well-known experience. In fact, you should probably go ahead and expect to feel this way a time or two as you walk through these eight weeks of study—if you haven't already! It happens to us all, particularly those of us who trust Christ with our lives. We often think we've devoted ourselves fully to Jesus only to fall short in a way that makes it obvious we still have far to go.

Disciples of Jesus follow Jesus, and following Jesus involves a lifelong path of learning and growth. It begins with Jesus's invitation to come and follow Him. It continues until our transformation is complete—and our transformation isn't complete until we are resurrected from this life to new life where we will dwell forever in God's magnificent glory. Until then, we take next steps to continue following Jesus right here and now—growing and learning to be more like Him along the way.

That's why each week of this study will include time for reflection and consideration of *Next Steps*. Jesus is calling you to come to Him and follow after Him. That invitation is ongoing. There will never be a day in your life when He will not extend that same offer. So take some time to reflect on what you've been studying and the next steps Jesus is leading you to take as you walk with Him. Let Him show you how you can become more fully devoted to Him.

The Word became flesh and dwelt among us. We observed his glory,
the glory as the one and only Son from the Father, full of grace and truth.
JOHN 1:14

Read John 1 in your Bible. Let it guide a time of prayerful reflection about devoting yourself fully to Jesus.

Record some next steps you'll take to answer Jesus's invitation to come follow Him.

Using the columns below—on the left, identify ways you're growing in Christ. On the right, identify the other ways you are seeking change, renewal, and repentance.

Growing	Changing

WEEK 2

BELIEVE IN ME

START

Welcome everyone to session 2, "Believe in Me."
Before introducing session 2, take a few minutes to review session 1.

Before we start digging into new content each week, we'll spend some time talking about what we've discovered or rediscovered during the previous week's personal study. The review questions will help us lean into the full devotion God wants us to know and experience in relationship with Him.

In what way do you need to "come" to Jesus? Is there a situation you've been trying to handle without accepting His invitation?

As we daily answer Jesus's invitation to come to Him, we realize there is always more He wants us to know and experience. We will never exhaust His desire for us to know Him more fully! This week, we're going to reflect on His greatest gift: salvation— the gift through which every other thing we believe in Him flows.

What have you believed in Jesus? What do you need to believe in Jesus?

To prepare for video session 2, pray together.
God, help each of us accept Your invitation to know that
Your grace is stronger, bigger, and greater than anything
we've ever done—and that it is being offered to us.

WATCH

Use this section to take notes as you watch video session 2.

Salvation is a gift we receive when we put our faith and trust in Jesus.

EPHESIANS 1:13

God can't become your Father and Jesus become your Lord and the Holy Spirit enter your heart and it not change you.

2 CORINTHIANS 5:17

As we grow in the Lord, there is evidence of increasing transformation.

1 JOHN 5:1; 2:3-6; 3:9-10,24

HEBREWS 12:7-11

DISCUSS

After viewing the video, discuss the following questions with your group.

Stephen asked, "Would you rather work for something, or would you rather someone who loves you give it to you?" How does a person's answer to that question impact their receiving of what God gives—salvation in Jesus Christ?

What is the root of salvation and the fruit of salvation? How are they different?

Read 2 Corinthians 5:17. If a person experiences transformation when they receive salvation in Christ, then in what sense is salvation a continuing process of growth over time? How have you seen that reality in your own life?

When did you first believe and receive God's gift of salvation in Jesus Christ? What led you to devote yourself to Jesus in that way? How has that decision changed your life?

Close in prayer.

Prayer Requests:

DAY 1
THE ANSWER YOU DESPERATELY NEED

Complete the following statements with the first thing that comes to your mind:

Without food, I am _____.

Without sleep, I am _____.

Without Jesus, I am _____.

It has been said that the first step to dealing with a problem is admitting you have one. Think about this: When you're tired and hungry, you feel the effects and look to correct the problem quickly, right? A spiritual deficiency, though, can often be misunderstood, overlooked, or altogether ignored.

We need to understand our dilemma without Christ. We tend to think we're *pretty bad off* without Jesus but there's no real present danger. That's because we compare and categorize sins. We think about things like our internet activity and reactions to other drivers in traffic as justifiable—after all, those aren't as bad as cheating on your spouse or murder. We start to think about people in categories that way, too. If a neighbor or coworker seems like a pretty good guy, we're not too worried about his soul.

In essence, what we're saying when we categorize and compare sins in that way is, *I don't think God really cares about this particular issue. It's small stuff— not a big deal.* And we grow apathetic about our own particular brand of sin. But Scripture tells a different story.

> *And you were dead in your trespasses and sins in which you previously walked according to the ways of this world, according to the ruler of the power of the air, the spirit now working in the disobedient. We too all previously lived among them in our fleshly desires, carrying out the inclinations of our flesh and thoughts, and we were by nature children under wrath as the others were also.*
> **EPHESIANS 2:1-3**

How does Ephesians 2 describe you and everyone you know?
- ☐ "pretty bad off" without Jesus
- ☐ under God's wrath and completely dead without Jesus

Why is it critical that you understand the depth of helplessness that defines all people apart from Christ?

We need to make a shift in our thinking. Sin isn't pretty bad—it *kills* the life God created us to have. Without Jesus, life isn't less than ideal—it's completely futile. Without understanding the depth of our need, there is no urgency or desperation for forgiveness and redemption.

Do you think of yourself as someone in desperate need of forgiveness? Why or why not?

Do you think of the people you encounter each day as sinners in desperate need of forgiveness? Why or why not?

You can't be fully devoted to Christ unless you know who you are without Him. Who you are without Him is someone with a problem that cannot be fixed. You are dead in your sins, whatever those sins are. All of us are. You need Jesus to save you. All of us do. He's the answer we desperately need.

What would you say to someone who says, "God knows I'm going to sin, so I might as well just live how I want and ask forgiveness later"?

Jesus is the answer you desperately need at every moment of your life. As you come to Him daily, you will continue to receive from Him the strength and grace you need to follow Him, fully devoted.

DAY 2
THE RANSOM YOU CAN'T PAY

If the first step to dealing with your spiritual need is admitting you have one, then admitting you can't fix that need on your own is the critical second.

What are some ways people wrongly try to repair their spiritual problems?

What do the following verses teach you about those efforts?

Romans 7:15-20

1 Peter 1:18-19

Acts 4:12

Understanding the depth of your need isn't enough. You need to understand your utter helplessness in meeting that need. Trying to be good enough to earn your salvation is a fool's errand. So is trusting in *any other name* than Jesus.

Jesus did for you what you cannot do. He lived the perfect life and died the perfect death. No one else ever has or ever will. He came to set you free and deliver you from the wrath of God. Jesus didn't just teach and model a good life, He gave His life as a ransom for sin—*your* sin and the sins of all who repent and believe in the gospel.

> *"For even the Son of Man did not come to be served,*
> *but to serve, and to give his life as a ransom for many."*
> **MARK 10:45**

The word *ransom* is telling. Jesus didn't simply come to earth to give you a nice gift. He came to give you His very *life* out of necessity. Your sin holds you captive—and your only hope for release is a payment you have no way of making. Who holds you captive? Hebrews 2:14-15 explains.

> *Now since the children have flesh and blood in common, Jesus also shared in these, so that through his death he might destroy the one holding the power of death—that is, the devil—and free those who were held in slavery all their lives by the fear of death.*
> **HEBREWS 2:14-15**

Read also 1 John 3:8. Apart from Christ, what power does the devil have over you?

What is the only way the devil loses that power over you?

Sin gave the devil a foothold in your life—and in your death. Sin always causes death. Knowing you are unable to overcome sin and death on your own, God sent Jesus to give His life on your behalf. Jesus came to pay your ransom in full. In His sacrificial death, He destroyed the devil's power over you. Jesus paid the ransom you can't pay and gives you everlasting *life* in return.

Read Colossians 2:13-15. List the victories Jesus accomplished on your behalf as He paid your ransom through His death.

> *For the wages of sin is death, but the gift of God is eternal life in Christ Jesus our Lord.*
> **ROMANS 6:23**

DAY 3
THE GIFT THAT'S GIVEN FREELY

Have you ever received a free gift—one that came without any action on your part and no expectation of exchange? Have you ever given a gift like that? Explain.

By definition, gifts are freely given. At the same time, though, we typically give and receive gifts with some sort of expectation. We exchange birthday gifts and Christmas gifts with hope for a certain response from the recipients. We sign up for giveaways and attend events that offer door prizes. In a sense, whether through friendship, position, or activity, the gifts we give and receive aren't truly free. They are earned through work, access, or relationship. Gifts that are truly free are rare.

Read Ephesians 2:4-9. What have you done to receive the gift of salvation in Jesus Christ?

Based on these verses, what does the free gift of salvation in Jesus Christ do for you?

God's gift to you in Jesus Christ is different than any other gift you could ever give or receive. This week, you've read about the despair of the old life, the one where you try to be good enough and work hard enough to earn God's favor. In that life, you are dead, enslaved, an object of wrath, disobedient, and under Satan's dominion (Ephesians 2:1-3). In that life, you have desperate need and owe a ransom you can't pay (Romans 6:23a). But don't miss the best part of the story! Jesus paid that ransom on your behalf with His life—as a gift in the truest sense of the word (Romans 6:23b).

How do you benefit from this gift that's given so freely? Read Ephesians 2:12-20 to complete the following sentences. Circle all that apply.

Without Christ's free gift of salvation, I am _____(v. 12).

included in God's family   *a foreigner to God's covenant promises*

without hope   *a citizen of God's eternal kingdom*

without God   *hopeful*   *excluded from God's family*

In receiving Christ's free gift of salvation, I am _____(vv.13-20).

near to God   *far from God*   *left on my own to please God*

at peace with God   *part of God's family*   *a spiritual outsider*

a fellow citizen with the saints   *given access to God*

being built together for God's dwelling in the Spirit

You don't need to do anything to receive Christ's gift of salvation, but in receiving that gift, changes take place. Have you received this free gift?

Jesus came for the world, and for you individually, to display the amazing gift of God's grace. Your old self becomes new, not because you "become good" or achieve something that God thinks is commendable. There's nothing to be proud of, except that God's goodness demonstrated itself on your behalf through Jesus's sacrifice on the cross. Salvation is received out of pure and unfailing love, a gift that comes of 100% unmerited favor.

For you are saved by grace through faith, and this is not from yourselves;
it is God's gift— not from works, so that no one can boast.
EPHESIANS 2:8-9

FULLY DEVOTED

DAY 4
THE FRIEND WHO IS WORTH FOLLOWING

This week, you've seen that you have a desperate need, and Jesus is the only right answer to that need. He paid the ransom you can't pay, and He offers that gift to you freely—which is great, because you can't possibly pay Jesus back. What you can do, though, is believe Him, receive His gift, and follow Him—and that's exactly what He's calling you to do.

> *"No one has greater love than this: to lay down his life for his friends. You are my friends if you do what I command you. I do not call you servants anymore, because a servant doesn't know what his master is doing. I have called you friends, because I have made known to you everything I have heard from my Father. You did not choose me, but I chose you. I appointed you to go and produce fruit and that your fruit should remain, so that whatever you ask the Father in my name, he will give you."*
> **JOHN 15:13-16**

What word does Jesus repeatedly use to describe those who believe, receive, and follow Him?

How has Jesus demonstrated your worth as His friend? How does He continue to demonstrate your worth as His friend?

How would a friend of Christ relate to Him differently than a servant of Christ?

36

Jesus does not call you to believe Him, receive His gift, and blindly follow Him as a dutiful servant who is given no insight, understanding, or answers to the questions that following Him most certainly brings. Because He loves you as a most-treasured friend, He enlightens, equips, and empowers you to walk in step with Him.

There is no greater love you can know than the love of Jesus. He considers you His friend, so much so that He sacrificed His life on the cross to enjoy relationship with you throughout eternity. Jesus is the friend who is worth following.

Read John 3:16-21. Based on verses 16-18, what two eternal outcomes are available to all people?

Based on verses 19-21, what two choices are before you today?

How do verses 19-21 help you understand what Jesus means by "believe" in verses 16-18?

In your own words, why is Jesus the friend who is worth following?

The One who proved His great love and eternal commitment to knowing you as a friend at the cross now calls you to believe in Him and receive His grace, sacrifice, and forgiveness. Such belief is more than a simple nod of the head in intellectual acknowledgment. It is a decision to daily step out of the darkness and into the light of God's power, fully devoted to Him through the life, death, and resurrection of Jesus Christ.

"But anyone who lives by the truth comes to the light, so that
his works may be shown to be accomplished by God."
JOHN 3:21

DAY 5
NEXT STEPS TO FOLLOW

A heart that's fully devoted to Jesus isn't something you can experience by association to anything or anyone but Jesus Himself. In other words, you can't inherit the faith of a parent like you inherit the color of your eyes or the shape of your nose. Neither can you piggyback your way to closeness with Christ through someone else's devotion to Him. In and of itself, going to church isn't a sign of salvation.

Before we go any further in our study, we must each acknowledge that relationship with Jesus is an individual choice. Apart from that choice, you will never receive in Christ the blessings of Christ.

> *Then Jesus said to the Jews who had believed him, "If you continue in my word, you really are my disciples. You will know the truth, and the truth will set you free."*
>
> *"We are descendants of Abraham," they answered him, "and we have never been enslaved to anyone. How can you say, 'You will become free'?"*
>
> *Jesus responded, "Truly I tell you, everyone who commits sin is a slave of sin. A slave does not remain in the household forever, but a son does remain forever. So if the Son sets you free, you really will be free."*
> **JOHN 8:31-36**

Jesus isn't only the answer *other people* desperately need and the ransom *other people* can't pay. He's the answer *you* desperately need and the ransom *you* can't pay. He's not only calling other people to believe and receive His free gift. He's calling you to believe and receive it. He's not just the friend worthy for other people to follow, while you stand aside and watch. He's the friend worthy for you to follow. Jesus lived, died, and rose from the grave for *you*. And He is calling you to believe and receive His sacrificial grace, forgiveness, and freedom.

Have you prayed an authentic prayer of belief in and devotion to Jesus Christ? Have you made that belief public in baptism? Jesus is calling you to receive His gift of salvation and to begin walking with Him in faith. This is where full devotion to God begins.

If you have received in Jesus God's grace, forgiveness, and freedom, consider this: Are you making that belief public in obedience to God's commands?

Record some next steps you'll take to answer Jesus's invitation to receive freedom in Him. Make two lists below. On the left, identify ways you're showing that you have personally made the choice to follow Jesus. On the right, identify ways you want to begin showing that choice more clearly.

Following	Showing More Clearly

WEEK 3

SURRENDER TO ME

START

Welcome everyone to session 3, "Surrender to Me."
Before introducing session 3, take a few minutes to review session 2.

As we did last week, we want to spend some time talking about what God has taught us in our personal study. As we consider what it means to be fully devoted to Jesus, we're finding out that He invites us to come to Him and believe in Him daily in increasing ways.

In what way do you need to believe in Jesus?

What next step did you identify that God is inviting you to take?

Every person who comes to Jesus to receive salvation from Him is forever changed. That change also involves an ongoing process of daily growth and transformation. That process in us is led by God's Spirit, and it also is a decision we must make. It involves the daily surrender of our human nature.

What is something you currently need to surrender to God?

To prepare for video session 3, pray together.

God, help each of us accept Your invitation to live in sync

with the fact that You are Lord and we are not.

WATCH

Use this section to take notes as you watch video session 3.

Jesus wants us to be "all in" as His disciples.

LUKE 9:23

When we do good things for our own glory, that's the only reward we'll ever get.

MATTHEW 6

When we surrender our lives to the Lord, He satisfies us in ways the world can't.

MATTHEW 13:44-46

EPHESIANS 3:20-21

DISCUSS

After viewing the video, discuss the following questions with your group.

Read Luke 9:23-25. Why is full devotion to Jesus not optional for believers? Why does receiving true salvation require fully surrendering to Him?

Why do you think Jesus commands us to take this action daily?

Read Matthew 6:1-8,16-18. Alex shared his struggle with having the right motivation for doing good things. He said he realized God was saying, "Choose." When have you felt this kind of tension within yourself?

Read Matthew 13:44-46. Why is surrendering everything to Jesus worth whatever cost comes with that decision?

Which areas of life, either now or in the past, have had you saying, "No, I can't surrender that," to Jesus? What's holding you back? What might it look like to allow God to speak to those areas this week?

Close in prayer.

Prayer Requests:

DAY 1
THE REASON TO BE "ALL IN"

When in your life have you been "all in" with something or someone?

Did your devotion ever fade, or have you remained "all in" from the start? Explain?

What are some reasons people might profess faith in Christ but not be "all in" and fully devoted to Him?

Throughout history and all over the world, God's people have struggled to consistently relate to Him in a way that is truly "all in." Many receive His free gift of grace but are soon tempted to take that grace for granted. Even when not consciously taken for granted, devotion to God often waxes and wanes with time and circumstance. Though it's not a new phenomenon, it is shortsighted every time.

While the apostle John was in exile at the end of his life, Jesus gave him messages of encouragement and warning to pass along to seven churches because they, too, were being tempted away from full devotion. Jesus's friends in Smyrna were impoverished, afflicted, and slandered—and their circumstances would get worse. Yet He wanted them to remain faithful in full devotion, no matter what.

> *"Don't be afraid of what you are about to suffer. Look, the devil is about to throw some of you into prison to test you, and you will experience affliction for ten days. Be faithful to the point of death, and I will give you the crown of life."*
> **REVELATION 2:10**

What fear or suffering has tempted you toward unfaithfulness to Jesus?

How does Revelation 2:10 encourage you to be "all in" with Jesus?

Jesus equips, encourages, and empowers His friends to be fully devoted to Him in every circumstance. But He won't force it. Just as believing in Jesus and receiving His gift of salvation is a matter of individual decision, so is the choice to remain "all in" when following Him proves difficult.

Read John 6:66-69. Why did Peter and the other disciples go "all in" with Jesus when others turned away?

Answer Jesus's question to the twelve disciples (v. 67) for yourself. What reason do you have to be fully devoted to Jesus?

Many will turn away from Jesus (Matthew 13:3-8,19-23). Some will continue to have an appearance of devotion, but the reality of their lives will more resemble the culture of the world than the commands of Christ. Their spiritual lives will be ineffective at best.

Jesus is calling you to be "all in"—to stay fully devoted to Him. That's what disciples do. And one day, every disciple of Jesus will join countless thousands of angels in heaven, declaring the reason why (Revelation 5:11-13). In the hardest teachings and in the most fearful situations, Jesus is worthy of your whole self and utmost devotion.

> *Worthy is the Lamb who was slaughtered*
> *to receive power and riches*
> *and wisdom and strength*
> *and honor and glory and blessing!*
> **REVELATION 5:12B**

What would change in your life this week if you were to be "all in," fully devoted to Jesus?

DAY 2
THE CONSIDERATION OF COST

"For which of you, wanting to build a tower, doesn't first sit down and calculate the cost to see if he has enough to complete it? Otherwise, after he has laid the foundation and cannot finish it, all the onlookers will begin to ridicule him, saying, 'This man started to build and wasn't able to finish.'"
LUKE 14:28-30

In this passage, Jesus wasn't giving His disciples a lesson on building a business in carpentry so they could make extra money with a side hustle. He was using an analogy to teach what it truly means to follow Him.

For more context, read Luke 14:25-27. Why would Jesus risk losing popularity and followers by speaking these difficult words to the crowd?

Salvation is received by grace through faith, not works (Ephesians 2:8-9). How, then, are Jesus's words in Luke 14:25-30 also true?

How might family commitments or other relational situations in your life sometimes hinder you from following Jesus with full devotion?

Jesus invites everyone to receive His free gift of salvation and follow Him, but we don't get to define what that means. He does. We don't follow Jesus on our terms— we follow Jesus on His terms. And His terms can only be described as full devotion. As such, following Jesus has consequences. It means you're deciding to prioritize Him above everything and everyone else.

"Or what king, going to war against another king, will not first sit down and decide if he is able with ten thousand to oppose the one who comes against him with twenty thousand? If not, while the other is still far off, he sends a delegation and asks for terms of peace. In the same way, therefore, every one of you who does not renounce all his possessions cannot be my disciple."
LUKE 14:31-33

Based on Luke 14:25-33, what decision are you making when you turn to Jesus in faith?

It costs you nothing to receive salvation. Yet, in receiving salvation, you surrender everything to Jesus, no matter the cost. It is a whatever-is-necessary type of commitment—a willingness to let go of family, friends, possessions, dreams, goals, and any other thing that is necessary to follow Him with full devotion. Jesus said there is no other way.

If you have made a decision to follow Christ, did you first consider the cost of surrendering your life to Him? What has the experience of following Jesus cost you along the way?

What danger is there in not considering the cost of following Jesus?

"Now, salt is good, but if salt should lose its taste, how will it be made salty? It isn't fit for the soil or for the manure pile; they throw it out. Let anyone who has ears to hear listen."
LUKE 14:34-35

Jesus wrapped up His point with a third analogy: Salt that isn't salty is useless. In the same way, so are Christ "followers" who aren't following Christ. Jesus wants you to be His disciple, fully devoted. He's calling and equipping you to finish the race in faith—no matter what that race entails.

DAY 3
THE DEATH OF SELF

What thoughts and/or feelings come to mind when you first hear vthe word "lose"?

No one wants to lose something they consider valuable. Yet that's exactly what going "all in" with Jesus impels us to do. Consider again Jesus's words in Revelation 2:10c: *Be faithful to the point of death, and I will give you the crown of life.* It's confusing, isn't it? Death for life? By definition, those two words are opposites! And that's the point. Jesus's command for us to be faithful to the point of death so that we gain life seems upside-down—and it should.

Relationship with Jesus is *different.* In fact, it's oxymoronic. The poor are rich (Matthew 5:3). You win by losing (Matthew 20:26). Strength comes through weakness (2 Corinthians 12:10). Freedom comes through bondage (Romans 6:22). When you lose your life, you find it (Matthew 16:25). The call to follow Jesus will often contradict everything you naturally think, feel, and reason. And that's *good.*

> *Then Jesus said to his disciples, "If anyone wants to follow after me, let him deny himself, take up his cross, and follow me. For whoever wants to save his life will lose it, but whoever loses his life because of me will find it. For what will it benefit someone if he gains the whole world yet loses his life? Or what will anyone give in exchange for his life?"*
> **MATTHEW 16:24-26**

How do denying yourself, taking up your cross, and following Jesus contradict our assumptions about how a person lives his or her best life?

What do Jesus's questions in verse 26 infer about those assumptions?

Living your best life *requires* a death to self. After all, that's what repentance is—turning away from what you and the rest of the world naturally think, feel, and reason and turning toward the way and will of God. We don't ask Him to step into our thoughts and plans; He tells us to step into His.

> Read Isaiah 55:8-9. Why will God's will often contradict yours?

Jesus didn't teach an easy believism, and He isn't interested in that type of follower. He wants us to understand that our thoughts and ways are sinful and His are perfect. He wants us to demonstrate that understanding by laying down our own lives to follow Him.

> *"Therefore produce fruit consistent with repentance."*
> **MATTHEW 3:8**

> In what situation are you currently following your will and way instead of God's?

> What would it look like for you to die to self in repentance?

> How can you make this part of your daily practice of following Jesus?

Repentance isn't a one-time deal that happens the day you first decide to follow Jesus. We must take up our cross daily (Luke 9:23). Discipleship, losing your life in favor of life in Christ, is an ongoing process of daily surrender. In surrendering your own will to follow God's will, you will find new life daily as your old self wastes away and more of Christ is born within you.

DAY 4
THE LAYING DOWN OF IDOLS

The call of total surrender is a hard topic. It's an even harder practice. But don't give up! The reality is that when you give God an "all in" type of commitment, no matter the cost, He gives you His presence, power, and provision as needed to help you continue—and receive a joyful reward as you do!

List a few things you fear following Jesus might require you to give up. Consider pursuits, relationships, interests, and priorities.

Place a check beside anything on your list that you are prone to prioritize more than God.

In this world full of distraction and temptation, God knew we'd struggle to give Him our full devotion—so much so that He began the Ten Commandments with two that speak to idolatry. He didn't do that only for people in those days who actually created physical objects to bow down to. He also gave them for the sake of people in our generation whose idols, though maybe harder to recognize, are no less prolific and harmful.

Read Exodus 20:3-6. What are the two commands?

Look again at the priorities you listed and then checked. Have you ever considered them idols? Why or why not? How do they impact your worship of God?

Yesterday, we read Jesus's command for us to lose our lives for Him. Losing your life means dying to self, and dying to self means laying down your idols. Throughout Scripture, God warns us about the destructiveness of those pursuits, relationships, and interests that we give fuller devotion to than Him. Consider the following three verses in the New Testament letters.

Little children, guard yourselves from idols.
1 JOHN 5:21

Therefore, put to death what belongs to your earthly nature: sexual immorality, impurity, lust, evil desire, and greed, which is idolatry.
COLOSSIANS 3:5

So then, my dear friends, flee from idolatry.
1 CORINTHIANS 10:14

What three directives do these verses give about idols in your life?

What are some ways you can guard yourself from idols?

What would it look like for you to "put to death" idolatry that already exists in your life?

Read 1 Corinthians 10:1-13. Why do you need to "flee" from idolatry?

Jesus's disciples follow Him with full devotion. And full devotion is far less about living a perfect life than it is about acknowledging daily your imperfection. It means recognizing your need for Jesus and relying on Him in complete surrender. Will you adopt a lifestyle of laying down your idols so that Jesus receives the honor and glory He is worthy to receive as you faithfully follow Him?

DAY 5
NEXT STEPS TO FOLLOW

So what does it look like practically to surrender your life to Jesus? What next steps do you need to take to follow Jesus with full devotion?

Take a look at the individual areas of your life and prayerfully consider what you have not fully surrendered to Jesus.

RELATIONSHIPS
(e.g., family, friendships, dating, marriage)

"If anyone comes to me and does not hate his own father and mother, wife and children, brothers and sisters— yes, and even his own life—he cannot be my disciple."
LUKE 14:26

SELF
(e.g., heart, mind, body, will, emotions)

"Whoever does not bear his own cross and come after me cannot be my disciple."
LUKE 14:27

POSSESSIONS
(e.g., houses, cars, things, money, time)

"In the same way, therefore, every one of you who does not renounce all his possessions cannot be my disciple."
LUKE 14:33

Ask and pray: What do I need to do to give You full devotion in these areas of my life?

Record some next steps you'll commit to take to present your life in full surrender to Jesus.

Therefore, brothers and sisters, in view of the mercies of God, I urge you to present your bodies as a living sacrifice, holy and pleasing to God; this is your true worship. Do not be conformed to this age, but be transformed by the renewing of your mind, so that you may discern what is the good, pleasing, and perfect will of God.
ROMANS 12:1-2

WEEK 4

ABIDE IN ME

START

Welcome everyone to session 4, "Abide in Me."
Before introducing session 4, take a few minutes to review session 3.

Before we jump into this week's study on what it means to abide in Jesus, let's talk about what we learned last week. In our personal study, we discovered that Jesus wants us to go "all in" with Him.

In what way do you need to surrender to Jesus?

What next step did you identify that God is inviting you to take?

As we surrender ourselves to God, we discover that decision is beautifully fruitful. What we give up in full devotion to God can't compare to what we gain as we abide in the gift of relationship Jesus offers.

What are some signs that show a person is abiding in Christ?

To prepare for video session 4, pray together.

God, help each of us accept Your invitation to stay in

intimate fellowship with Jesus all the time.

WATCH

Use this section to take notes as you watch video session 4.

The Christian life is not us trying to do great things for God. It is God doing great things through us as He strengthens us in the power of His Spirit.

JOHN 15:4-5

Some elements of abiding in Christ are confession, knowing and obeying God's Word, prayer, and loving others.

JOHN 15:1-17

A person who abides in Christ knows and shows love, joy, and the fruit of good works.

JOHN 15:8-11

DISCUSS

After viewing the video, discuss the following questions with your group.

Alex pointed out that it's easy for us to think it's up to us to live out the Christian life. How have you struggled with doing things for Jesus instead of abiding in Him?

Read John 15:1-17. Do Jesus's words here emphasize doing or being? Explain. What lesson does that have for us as His disciples?

Why do you need to abide in Christ?

What are some ways to abide in Christ? To what degree does that require our active participation?

How do Jesus's words in John 15 free you to be in Christ rather than living your life as someone who must do for Christ?

Close in prayer.

Prayer Requests:

DAY 1
THE REALITY OF DEVOTION

Have you ever tried to do something and failed miserably? What caused that failure?

It happens to all of us, in a variety of pursuits. Maybe you went to the golf course with a potential business partner—and by the 10th hole, you'd hit every golf ball you brought into the woods and water. Or maybe you found a recipe to bake a birthday cake that looks just like a bunny, which your 5-year-old would have loved—but your attempt at that bunny turned out looking more like a snowman who had melted away in the sun. The fact is, sometimes what we want to do, we do not do.

What about your relationship with the Lord? Is there an area of obedience in which you haven't found consistency? Why?

Read Galatians 5:16-18. Why do well-meaning believers struggle to obey God in the ways they have devoted themselves to obey?

In Romans 7:14-25, Paul expressed this as a personal reality. Does this mean that Paul was unable to devote himself fully to God? Are you?

You will not remain fully devoted to God by your own determination, ability, or strength. Salvation is received by grace through faith, not by works—and, positionally, you remain God's child in that same grace. In practice, however, your sin nature will choose to follow its own will over God's will every time. The only way to reconcile the tension between position and practice is to daily choose Christ and walk in the power of His Spirit.

Read John 15:1-11. What does Jesus teach here about your position as His child?

Count the number of times Jesus uses the word "remain" (your translation may use the word "abide") in this passage. What does His emphasis on remaining teach you about the practice of obeying His commands?

What does it mean for Jesus to remain in you?

What practical steps do you take to remain in Him?

Why does living in full devotion to God necessitate both you remaining in Jesus and Jesus remaining in you?

The words *remain* or *abide* appear ten or eleven times in this passage, depending on the translation. Not only that, but John used the word *remain* forty times in his Gospel and twenty-seven more times in his letters.[1] The repetition of that word emphasizes our need to rest in Jesus, to lean and depend entirely on Him in order to live out the practice of life in Him.

You can't do it on your own! Staying connected to Jesus is a critical aspect of full devotion. You must continually choose to accept His daily invitation to walk with Him, learn from Him, and obey His Word.

> *"Remain in me, and I in you. Just as a branch is unable to produce fruit by itself unless it remains on the vine, neither can you unless you remain in me."*
> **JOHN 15:4**

---

1. Kenneth O. Gangel, John, vol. 4, Holman New Testament Commentary (Nashville, TN: Broadman & Holman Publishers, 2000), 283.

DAY 2
THE DECISION OF DISCIPLESHIP

In the 1991 movie *City Slickers*, there's a scene where a businessman named Mitch (who is facing a mid-life existential crisis) and a rough cowboy named Curly ride side-by-side on horses, discussing the meaning of life. Curly says, "You spend about fifty weeks a year getting knots in your rope, and then you think two weeks up here will untie them for ya. None of you get it. Do you know what the secret of life is?" Mitch admits, "No, what?" Curly holds up an index finger and says, "This. One thing. Just one thing." Mitch asks, "That's great, but what's the one thing?" Curly smiles and explains, "That's what you've gotta figure out."

Based on what you've learned in this study so far, what would you say is the meaning of life?

Unlike Curly in *City Slickers*, Jesus doesn't make us figure out what that one thing is. He teaches us again and again in His Word through direct instruction, illustrative stories, and personal interactions that our one thing is pursuing Him: coming to Him, receiving from Him, surrendering to Him, and abiding in Him. Consider Luke's account of Jesus and two sisters named Mary and Martha.

> *While they were traveling, he entered a village, and a woman named Martha welcomed him into her home. She had a sister named Mary, who also sat at the Lord's feet and was listening to what he said. But Martha was distracted by her many tasks, and she came up and asked, "Lord, don't you care that my sister has left me to serve alone? So tell her to give me a hand." The Lord answered her, "Martha, Martha, you are worried and upset about many things, but one thing is necessary. Mary has made the right choice, and it will not be taken away from her."*
> **LUKE 10:38-42**

Underline what Mary chose that was the "one thing" Martha needed.

What distracted Martha from the one thing that she needed?

When Jesus arrived at the house that day, Mary and Martha each had a choice to make: to busily tend to tasks or to fully enjoy Jesus. It wasn't that taking care of her tasks was wrong, it was that her devotion to those tasks exceeded her desire to know and learn from Jesus. In choosing busyness, Martha confused her priorities.

What do Jesus's words to Martha in Luke 10 teach you about the secret of life?

What distracts you from choosing to enjoy intimacy with Jesus?

We have the same choice before us each day that Mary and Martha did. We choose distraction or discipleship, pursuits that have only earthly effect or pursuits that have eternal effect, to do *for* Christ or to be *in* Christ. Such is the decision of discipleship.

Without the opportunity to literally sit at Jesus's physical feet, what are some practical ways to make the one necessary and right choice that Mary did?

What changes would take place in your life this week if you were to daily make the decision of discipleship?

DAY 3
THE POWER OF HIS SPIRIT

It's true that devoting ourselves to Jesus is a decision we make with intention (Luke 10:42). It's also true that being fully devoted to Jesus isn't something we can carry out ourselves, even with the very best of intentions (Romans 7:21). It's a conundrum! But even the greatest opposing realities that coexist within us are met with divine provision. God has given us Himself to equip and empower us to follow Him, fully devoted.

"When the Counselor comes, the one I will send to you from the Father —
the Spirit of truth who proceeds from the Father—he will testify about me."
JOHN 15:26

Consider the words "truth," "from the Father," and "testify" in light of the Spirit who indwells all who follow Jesus. Name a situation in which your devotion to Jesus might falter. What truth about Jesus do you need God's Spirit to testify to you in that situation?

When has God equipped and empowered you to follow Him when, in your own strength, you wouldn't have been able to remain fully devoted?

What do personal experience and the fact that the Spirit of truth within you "proceeds from the Father" tell you about your potential to remain fully devoted?

Jesus sent His Spirit to dwell within all believers, equipping and empowering us to do the work He has called us to do. And He Himself ensures our ability to carry out that work. So we should not minimize the role God has given us. Neither should we underestimate His Spirit's power within us. We are Christ's witnesses, supernaturally declaring and demonstrating the message of salvation to unbelievers. The Holy Spirit testifies to the world the glorious gospel message that Jesus Christ is the Messiah through imperfect people like you who rely on His perfect strength in their own weaknesses.

We learned in day two of this week's study that full devotion to Christ— and experiencing all the blessings of that relationship—is, in part, a decision we make. Similarly, Ephesians 5:18 instructs us to "be filled by the Spirit." What steps can you take to allow the Spirit to fill you?

It was as difficult for the believers in Ephesus to remain fully devoted to Jesus as it is for believers in our day—maybe even more so. Their culture was marked by ritualistic pagan worship that encouraged drunkenness as a way of communing with the gods. Paul wanted them to know the God of heaven is different. To worship Him, you must submit yourself to His Spirit. As we yield ourselves to the power of God's Spirit, He fills us and leads us to know God's will and faithfully serve Him.[1]

> *But the fruit of the Spirit is love, joy, peace, patience, kindness, goodness, faithfulness, gentleness, and self-control. The law is not against such things. Now those who belong to Christ Jesus have crucified the flesh with its passions and desires. If we live by the Spirit, let us also keep in step with the Spirit.*
> **GALATIANS 5:22-25**

What does Galatians 5:22-25 teach you about being fully devoted to God?

---

1. Max Anders, Galatians-Colossians, vol. 8, Holman New Testament Commentary (Nashville, TN: Broadman & Holman Publishers, 1999), 172.

DAY 4
THE HEART OF THE MATTER

Based on this week's study, how can you best describe a person who is fully devoted to God?

- ☐ Someone who always obeys God's commands
- ☐ Someone who serves the church in a way that people see and admire
- ☐ Someone whose life is consistent with whatever they believe about God
- ☐ Someone who, though imperfect, believes the gospel, authentically holds on to Jesus, and continually invites the Spirit to direct his or her life

You can do many good things without being fully devoted to the Lord. You can live what you say you believe and never live in the power of God's Spirit. You can even be admired by other believers and still completely miss out on an authentic and growing relationship with Jesus. That was a reality for people in Jesus's day, and it is a reality now.

Read Luke 8:1-8. Jesus was preaching the good news of God's kingdom, and people were responding and following Him. Why was it the right moment for Jesus to tell this parable?

Why is this an important parable for you to hear and listen to in a study about being fully devoted to Jesus?

Just as farmers sow seeds with differing results depending on the soil they land on, Jesus sowed seeds of truth as He preached the good news of God's kingdom that would have different results depending on the heart of each listener. Jesus is also doing that right now, in this very moment. In short, the effect of these weeks of study is dependent upon the condition of your heart.

Read Luke 8:9-15. Carefully consider the four heart conditions Jesus describes. As you do, check the one that best reflects the current condition of your heart.

- ☐ HARD: hears God's Word but its truth is easily stolen and replaced by Satan's lies
- ☐ ROCKY: receives God's Word with joy but grows no roots and does not continue in that joy when tough times come
- ☐ THORNY: does not give attention to understanding and applying God's Word so earthly pursuits overtake any potential for spiritual fruit
- ☐ GOOD: hears, welcomes, receives, and grows in God's Word to the point of fruitful effect in the various circumstances of life

"But the seed in the good ground—these are the ones who, having heard the word with an honest and good heart, hold on to it and by enduring, produce fruit."
LUKE 8:15

Now, halfway through a study called *Fully Devoted*, we each need to check our hearts. Jesus teaches us that participation does not guarantee spiritual effect. The reality is that all of us must acknowledge and confront the temptation that will certainly come our way.

You will be tempted to walk away from this study unchanged. Hearing or reading these truths will only draw you to Jesus if you turn your heart toward Him as an ongoing decision of faith.

What things in your life sometimes push out the Word of God?

What needs to change so that you might be more open and attentive to receiving the Word of God and continuing in it with your whole heart?

DAY 5
NEXT STEPS TO FOLLOW

We're at the midpoint in this study, but the choice to fully devote ourselves to Jesus is just beginning! His invitation to come, receive, surrender, and abide in Him will have no end. As a way of agreeing with Jesus in your understanding of that invitation, take some time now to reflect on what you've learned. Meditate on these key verses. Write them on note cards, and work to memorize them in the days ahead.

COME TO ME

"Come to me, all of you who are weary and
burdened, and I will give you rest."
MATTHEW 11:28

RECEIVE FROM ME

For the wages of sin is death, but the gift of God
is eternal life in Christ Jesus our Lord.
ROMANS 6:23

SURRENDER TO ME

Then Jesus said to his disciples, "If anyone wants to follow after
me, let him deny himself, take up his cross, and follow me.
MATTHEW 16:24

ABIDE IN ME

"I am the vine; you are the branches. The one who remains in me and I
in him produces much fruit, because you can do nothing without me."
JOHN 15:5

Record some next steps you'll take to answer Jesus's invitation to come, receive, surrender, and abide in Him.

Make two lists below. On the left, identify ways you're growing in Christ. On the right, identify the other ways you are seeking change, renewal, and repentance.

Growing	Changing

Week 5

SENT IN ME

START

Welcome everyone to session 5, "Sent in Me."
Before introducing session 5, take a few minutes to review session 4.

In last week's session, we saw seeking the gift of God's presence is essential to being fully devoted to Jesus. As we daily choose to abide in Jesus, who daily abides in us, we get to live in true relationship with Him.

In what situation do you need to "abide" in Jesus?

What next step did you identify that God is inviting you to take?

One of the fruits of abiding in Jesus is the impact He makes on other people's lives through us. We're not blessed with God's abiding presence simply to be blessed. We're given that grace to represent Him to the people around us. Our relationship with Him impacts how we see ourselves and other people.

What does it mean for you to be an ambassador for Christ?

To prepare for video session 5, pray together.
God, help each of us accept Your invitation to see and relate
to people around us with the compassion of Jesus.

WATCH

Use this section to take notes as you watch video session 5.

As we surrender to Jesus and abide in Him, He causes us to care about and love other people, wanting them to come to know the Lord.

MATTHEW 9:36-38

In Christ, our love for other people is bigger than the differences we have with them.

JOHN 4:7-42

We should ask God for opportunities to share the gospel with gentleness and respect and for people to receive salvation in Jesus.

EPHESIANS 6:19-20

DISCUSS

After viewing the video, discuss the following questions with your group.

Aside from physical appearance, what is the first thing you tend to notice about a person? Does that impact the way you relate to them? Explain. Based on the story of Jesus and the Samaritan woman in John 4, what was the first thing Jesus noticed about people? How should that impact us?

Read Matthew 9:35-38. What prompted Jesus to teach His disciples to pray for workers in God's kingdom harvest? What prompts you to pray for people to know Jesus and be saved?

Alex pointed out that we need to view people the way God wants us to view them. How does God want us to view other people? What tension is there in that for you?

Read Colossians 4:2-6. Paul didn't seem to have a hang-up about telling others about Jesus. He regularly shared the gospel with people he encountered. What, then, do Paul's requests in Colossians 4 teach us about being sent by Jesus?

Close in prayer.

Prayer Requests:

DAY 1
THE NEED FOR SPIRITUAL SIGHT

When has your perception and understanding of someone significantly changed after getting to know them better?

What factors contributed to this shift in your perspective?

Left to our own intellect and wisdom, we are more often wrong than right about other people. Our human perceptions are limited by what we can see and what we have personally experienced. And when our perceptions are limited, our love for people usually is, too. We need a shift in the way we view people. We need Jesus to give us spiritual sight.

Read the following verses and record in the first column what Jesus saw in the crowds He encountered. In the second column, record what Jesus did as a result.

	WHAT JESUS SAW	WHAT JESUS DID
Matthew 9:36-38		
Mark 6:34		
John 9:1-7		
John 10:11-18		

Based on Jesus's example, what shift in perspective do you need regarding the people you encounter each day?

We need a shift in mindset. We need to think differently. The person who is fully devoted to Jesus seeks to see and respond to people in the way of Jesus. And the way of Jesus is to see people with compassion, as sheep without a shepherd.

That's part of being Christ's disciple—learning to be more concerned about the condition of a person's soul than whether or not that person adds value to your earthly life. Without the love of Christ, you will never relate to people in the way of Christ. You will only come across as a noisy gong or clanging cymbal (1 Corinthians 13:1).

Read Matthew 14:15-17, 19:13-15 and John 4:27. How would you summarize the perspective Jesus's disciples had about people?

Now, read Acts 3:1-10. What shift had taken place in Peter and John's perspective?

How can you get better at noticing the opportunities God gives you to love others?

When he saw the crowds, he felt compassion for them, because they were distressed and dejected, like sheep without a shepherd. Then he said to his disciples, "The harvest is abundant, but the workers are few. Therefore, pray to the Lord of the harvest to send out workers into his harvest."
MATTHEW 9:36-38

DAY 2
THE NEED FOR THE GOSPEL GLOBALLY

I've never needed Jesus more than I do right now. That's a sentiment that has been expressed through the years in song lyrics, sermon manuscripts, and personal testimonies. To be clear, it is vitally important that we acknowledge our desperate need for Christ in difficult seasons. At the same time, there is a greater truth that exists beyond our feelings or challenging circumstances: All of us need Jesus all the time.

For all have sinned and fall short of the glory of God . . .
ROMANS 3:23

What one thing can you know is true about every single person alive in the world today, no matter their earthly circumstances?

In the cultural context of the community where you live and work, is the need for the gospel readily apparent to you? Mark an X on the continuum below to rate how often you recognize spiritual need in the day-to-day.

Never   Sometimes   Always

When you recognize spiritual needs around you, what usually causes that recognition to take place?

When you don't recognize spiritual needs around you, what prevents that from happening?

All around the globe, people need Jesus. That's true on the hardest days when world events make you especially aware and also on simpler days when life seems especially good. It's true in your home and all the way down your street. It's true in your workplace and every other place you go. It's also true in parts of the world you've never visited.

You might be thinking, "So what? If everyone everywhere needs the gospel, what good does it do for me to recognize that overwhelming and depressing reality?" Notice the sentence that begins in Romans 3:23 is incomplete. Let's look at the second half of the sentence recorded in verse 24 and revisit again the incredible truth we ourselves have come to receive, surrender to, and abide in.

> *. . . they are justified freely by his grace through*
> *the redemption that is in Christ Jesus.*
> **ROMANS 3:24**

You recognizing the global need for the gospel matters because everyone everywhere needs those who have received Christ's redemption to share their knowledge of that incredible gift. They need someone to share the gospel with them. They need *you*. Without hearing and receiving the gospel, they will die in their sins (John 8:24b). And Jesus has sent you to them—on hard days and good days, in your home and all the way down your street, in your workplace and every other place you go, and even in parts of the world you'll never physically visit.

> *Then he said to them, "Go into all the world and*
> *preach the gospel to all creation."*
> **MARK 16:15**

Read also Matthew 28:18-20. Why did Jesus lead His command with a statement of His authority and end it with the promise of His presence? How do those two bookends encourage you as you consider your role in meeting the global need for the gospel?

In addition to sharing the gospel with people you know, what are some practical ways you can answer Christ's call to step into this great need?

DAY 3
THE NEED FOR GOSPEL INTENTION

See if you can relate to these statistics: More than 9 in 10 Christians say they are open to having a conversation about faith with a friend. Similarly, 8 in 10 say they are open to having a conversation about faith with a stranger. About 60% have prayed in the past month for the salvation of a family member or friend. Yet in the past 6 months, far fewer Christians have shared the gospel with a friend (38%) or a stranger (30%).[1]

Are these statistics surprising to you? Why?

The fact is, you can know what Jesus calls you to do as His follower and let days, weeks, months, and even years pass without acting on that knowledge. In Luke 10, Jesus wanted to make sure His disciples knew that whatever faith they had must demonstrate itself in works—particularly in the work of sharing the gospel.

Read Luke 10:1-9. What did Jesus send His disciples out to do?

Read verses 17-24. What happened when the disciples had gospel conversations?

When the disciples did what Jesus commissioned them to do, the power of the gospel was made clear. And it made some uncomfortable—particularly those who had vast knowledge of the law but no real love for the One who created the law.

---

1. Earls, Aaron. "Christians Say They're Seeking but Not Having Evangelistic Conversations." Lifeway Research. Lifeway Christian Resources, May 24, 2022. https://research.lifeway.com/2022/05/24/christians-say-theyre-seeking-but-not-having-evangelistic-conversations/.

A lawyer who was a devout Jew challenged Jesus, thinking he could rightly diminish the power that was being displayed.

> *Then an expert in the law stood up to test him, saying,*
> *"Teacher, what must I do to inherit eternal life?"*
> *"What is written in the law?" he asked him. "How do you read it?"*
> *He answered, "Love the Lord your God with all your heart, with all your soul, with*
> *all your strength, and with all your mind," and "your neighbor as yourself."*
> *"You've answered correctly," he told him. "Do this and you will live."*
> **LUKE 10:25-28**

What two ways do those who are fully devoted to God demonstrate that devotion?

Knowing the lawyer didn't truly understand what it means to love God and people, Jesus next told a story about a Samaritan who took time and intention to help a man in need while others who knew God's law passed him by (Luke 10:29-37).

What about you? Do you walk by, or have you been helping? Are you simply open to sharing the gospel, or are you sharing the gospel? We love God and love people by meeting needs, and the greatest need of all people is salvation.

Read 1 Corinthians 9:22-27. How does Paul's analogy help you understand what makes the difference between being open to having gospel conversations and actually having gospel conversations?

What intentional action(s) can you take this week to move from simply being open to sharing the gospel to actually sharing the gospel?

> *Don't you know that the runners in a stadium all race, but only*
> *one receives the prize? Run in such a way to win the prize.*
> **1 CORINTHIANS 9:24**

DAY 4
THE NEED FOR AUTHENTIC FAITH

The world is becoming more and more skeptical about people who say they follow Jesus. For example, while they're open to learning about faith in Christ,the majority of Gen Z only wants to learn from teachers who keep it real. In their view, the gospel fails to offer authentic hope when the person preaching the gospel appears one way on stage and is completely different in real life. They don't expect teachers to be perfect in their obedience to Christ's commands; they really just want people to be honest about their struggles in the faith and how we deal with those struggles.[1]

> *What good is it, my brothers and sisters, if someone claims to have*
> *faith but does not have works? Can such faith save him?*
> **JAMES 2:14**

In your own words, what point is James making in this verse?

What are some actions that coincide with genuine faith?

Essentially, James 2:14 teaches us that genuine faith drives us to action. If it doesn't, then it's not really faith at all. One action that accompanies genuine faith is sharing the gospel. Those who are living by faith are not ashamed of the gospel; instead, they readily share the gospel because they know it is the only way people can be saved (Romans 1:15-17).

---

1. Lykins, Liz. "Gen Z Christians Want Leaders to Keep It Real." Christianity Today. March 24, 2023. https://www.christianitytoday.com/news/2023/march/gen-z-christian-faith-pastors-church-generation-authentic.html.

Read James 2:14-26. Based on these verses, how would you describe genuine faith?

Does this mean the way to be saved is to do good deeds like helping people and sharing the gospel? How can you tell whether your actions are an attempt to earn salvation or the result of having received salvation?

What is the connection between authentic faith and sharing the gospel?

Your faith does not require works as a means of justifying you before God or people. Rather, works are a required response to the salvation you receive by faith alone (see again Ephesians 2:8-10). You don't have to tell people about Jesus for Jesus to save you, but when Jesus saves you, you'll want to tell people about Him! And your faith-driven actions will help others recognize the power of the gospel.

Unbelievers don't need to see you as a perfect person—you're not, and they'll know it. They need to see you as an imperfect person whom Jesus is transforming. And if you have received the gift of salvation, that is exactly who you are!

Based on James 2:14-26, how would you describe your faith? Is it genuine or disingenuous?

Where might God be calling you to demonstrate your faith?

With that in mind, what do you need to do to help people know you are an imperfect person being transformed by Jesus?

Let love be without hypocrisy. Detest evil; cling to what is good.
ROMANS 12:9

DAY 5
NEXT STEPS

Jesus is calling you to be sent in Him. Those who truly answer that call don't consider it a perfunctory duty but an honored privilege. You are sent in Jesus with a heart of love for God and people. One important way to grow in your love for God and people is to pray with that intention.

But I tell you, love your enemies and pray for those who persecute you.
MATTHEW 5:44

Who is someone hard to like that you need to learn to love?

First of all, then, I urge that petitions, prayers, intercessions,
and thanksgivings be made for everyone.
1 TIMOTHY 2:1

In what context does your spiritual sight need to improve (e.g., in how you see family members, coworkers, neighbors, other people in your community of faith, day-to-day acquaintances, people around the world)?

Then he said to his disciples, "The harvest is abundant,
but the workers are few. Therefore, pray to the Lord
of the harvest to send out workers into his harvest."
MATTHEW 9:37-38

How is prayer meant to impact your heart for God and others?

Based on your answers to the previous questions, use the space below to journal a prayer to God. Confess your need to develop spiritual eyesight and grow in love for God and people. Ask God to create in you a heart that genuinely longs to see other people come to salvation and to give you the courage to live with gospel intention.

Brothers and sisters, my heart's desire and prayer
to God concerning them is for their salvation.
ROMANS 10:1

WEEK 6

LOVE LIKE ME

START

Welcome everyone to session 6, "Love Like Me."
Before introducing session 6, take a few minutes to review session 5.

If these weekly sessions seem to be building on the previous ones, that's because they are! As we come to Jesus, receiving, surrendering to, and abiding in His grace, He causes those inward changes to produce outward effect. We saw that He helps us see other people like He does—with compassion for them in their deep, spiritual need.

What qualities would indicate someone is "sent in Jesus"?

What next step did you identify that God is inviting you to take?

When we see people like Jesus does, we begin to relate to them like Jesus does—in love. This week, we'll see what that looks like. What does it mean to love people like Jesus does?

What is your gut response to this week's title, "Love Like Me"? Would you say that you love a lot of people or a close-knit few? Why?

To prepare for video session 6, pray together.
God, help each of us accept Your invitation to walk
in loving community and relationships.

WATCH

Use this section to take notes as you watch video session 6.

The first church established community as Jesus modeled—before they tried to reach beyond their walls.

ACTS 2:42-47

Sometimes people will disappoint you, but no matter the cause, we must stay right with God and choose to forgive.

1 JOHN 2:9-11

We don't reach the world alone—we build community. But gospel community is filled with sinful, broken people, so we have to walk in love.

MATTHEW 10:5-8

DISCUSS

After viewing the video, discuss the following questions with your group.

What are some ways love is defined in our culture? Read Luke 10:25-37. Based on this passage, what does it mean to love like Jesus does?

Alex said, "Jesus modeled community by establishing loving relationships, and before He began to reach the world, He built a team." Why is it important for us to establish loving community in the church before we try to reach beyond our walls? What is challenging about that? What's exciting about it?

How has loving community played a role in your devotion to Jesus?

Based on the video teaching, how should you respond to someone who says, "The church is full of hypocrites. I'll follow Jesus on my own"?

Alex and Stephen named a lot of really practical ways we can love each other like Jesus. Which stood out to you? Why?

Close in prayer.

Prayer Requests:

DAY 1
THE REALITY OF LOVE

Fill in the blank: Love is _____.

Love is blind. It is also a battlefield, more than a feeling, and all you need. At least, those are some ways popular music has expressed love's meaning. Considering the fact that you were asked to define love in the context of a Bible study, you might have filled in the blank with something you've learned in Scripture—Love is God, the greatest commandment, or patient and kind.

Love can be described many ways. Even pop culture makes some excellent points. But for the purpose of growing as a disciple, we need to consider the word in terms of full devotion to Jesus, and in that context, love is a verb. It requires *action*.

> *Because if anyone is a hearer of the word and not a doer, he is like someone looking at his own face in a mirror. For he looks at himself, goes away, and immediately forgets what kind of person he was. But the one who looks intently into the perfect law of freedom and perseveres in it, and is not a forgetful hearer but a doer who works—this person will be blessed in what he does.*
> **JAMES 1:23-25**

For the past five weeks, you've been a "hearer" of the Word as you've been working through this study. Name a few important truths you've learned.

In the passage above, place brackets around the way James describes you if you don't act on what you've learned. Underline the way he describes you if you do.

Discipleship is a lifelong process. You will continually grow in your knowledge of truth and always have steps God wants you to take to put your faith into practice. Full devotion to Jesus has no end, even beyond this life.

Paul shares a similar truth to James 1:23-25 related to the topic of loving people like Jesus does:

If I speak human or angelic tongues but do not have love, I am a noisy gong or a clanging cymbal. If I have the gift of prophecy and understand all mysteries and all knowledge, and if I have all faith so that I can move mountains but do not have love, I am nothing. And if I give away all my possessions, and if I give over my body in order to boast but do not have love, I gain nothing.

Love is patient, love is kind. Love does not envy, is not boastful, is not arrogant, is not rude, is not self-seeking, is not irritable, and does not keep a record of wrongs. Love finds no joy in unrighteousness but rejoices in the truth. It bears all things, believes all things, hopes all things, endures all things.
1 CORINTHIANS 13:1-7

Paul didn't write this passage for a wedding. The reality of love goes far beyond one relationship in your life; it extends to all of them. Paul wrote these words for the church—disciples following Jesus together in real and messy relationships. Being fully devoted to Jesus means being fully devoted to other Christians.

Based on the truths expressed in 1 Corinthians 13:1-7 and James 1:23-25, complete the following sentence with a statement of action:

If I truly love God and follow Jesus, I will . . .

You learned in week five that the call of discipleship is also the call to go and make disciples. The call to go and make disciples means you must be in relationships with people, loving them in action as you step out of your comfort zone to meet needs and open your life to them in honest vulnerability. Being fully devoted to Jesus means inviting others to be fully devoted to Jesus alongside you.

Little children, let us not love in word or speech, but in action and in truth.
1 JOHN 3:18

DAY 2
THE UNITY OF FELLOWSHIP

It's fun to hang out with people you love. It's even more fun to hang out with people you *like*.

> Which has been most normative in your experience with other believers—learning to love people you like or learning to like people you are committed to love? What reason is there for that reality?

> How can you learn to like people you've committed to love?

In church life, we know we're supposed to love each other. And we were reminded in yesterday's study that love requires action. Consider those two truths in the context of the early church as described in Acts 2:41-42. In verse 41, we see three thousand people from various places came to faith in Christ in one day, and the very next verse infers relationships began immediately.

> *They devoted themselves to the apostles' teaching, to the*
> *fellowship, to the breaking of bread, and to prayer.*
> **ACTS 2:42**

> Based on the sequence of events in Acts 2:41-42, how would you characterize the first Christians? Did they learn to love people they liked or to like people they loved? What's the difference?

The effect of these believers' devotion to God and each other had profound eternal effect. The ways they actively loved and liked each other was so compelling that new disciples were made and joined their group every single day (Acts 2:47).

The kind of fellowship described in Acts is love showing itself in action. All Christians share a bond of purpose and devotion to Christ and each other. That bond of love impels friendship—the kind where we are bonded in the daily process of life.

How might the early believers' active devotion to fellowship have contributed to the process of learning to genuinely like each other?

How might a person's lack of engagement in fellowship with other believers negatively impact his or her effectiveness as a disciple maker?

It's not just fun to hang out with other believers in authentic fellowship—it's essential. Your own discipleship and your effectiveness as a discipler depends on it. Agreeing that you should love the body of Christ is only the beginning. Enjoying fellowship with one or two church members is a start. But don't stop there! Your spiritual growth and the spiritual growth of others require that you actively devote yourself to fellowship within the larger community of faith.

> *If we walk in the light as he himself is in the light, we have fellowship with one another, and the blood of Jesus his Son cleanses us from all sin.*
> **1 JOHN 1:7**

What promise is there about your relationships with other believers as you follow Jesus as His disciple?

What promise is there about your relationship with God as you follow Jesus as His disciple?

How does walking in the light draw us into fellowship with others?

DAY 3
THE GRACE OF SERVICE

**What is the most loving thing another person has done for you?
Why did they do it?**

Serving is a practice that is encouraged and celebrated by believers and unbelievers alike. Many high schools require the completion of service hours as a prerequisite for graduation. College clubs and organizations often center their activities around service. Communities plan events like walks, runs, and festivals to benefit service organizations. People of every religion, and even those who adhere to no religion at all, are compelled to serve others. Meeting needs is a widely shared value.

So what makes Jesus's call to serve different?

*For you were called to be free, brothers and sisters; only don't use this freedom
as an opportunity for the flesh, but serve one another through love. For the
whole law is fulfilled in one statement: Love your neighbor as yourself.*
GALATIANS 5:13-14

**What was Paul afraid the freedom the Galatians had received in Christ would
tempt them to do?**

Having received Jesus's invitation to come to Him for salvation by grace through faith alone, Gentile believers were tempted towards thinking they were released from any moral restraint. Meanwhile, Jewish believers were tempted towards establishing legalistic expectations like circumcision on Gentile believers. Both views were incorrect applications of the gospel message.

How does freedom in Christ compel us to serve others?

Jesus's call to service is reflective of your position of being made free in Him. It's not a performative expectation of acting in ways that earn His favor. It's more about being than doing. It's about sacrificial love, not self-serving duty.

> *Jesus called them over and said to them, "You know that those who are regarded as rulers of the Gentiles lord it over them, and those in high positions act as tyrants over them. But it is not so among you. On the contrary, whoever wants to become great among you will be your servant, and whoever wants to be first among you will be a slave to all. For even the Son of Man did not come to be served, but to serve, and to give his life as a ransom for many."*
> **MARK 10:42-45**

List examples of service from Jesus's earthly ministry.

What is extraordinary about Jesus coming to serve and not to be served?

In the process of personal discipleship and also in discipling others, Jesus is our example. He is Lord and King of the universe, yet He came to earth not to be served but to serve sinners at their point of need.

When we serve others in the way of Jesus and according to His power, He demonstrates through us the greatest form of love. That's because our doing good for others is, ultimately, a way to extend God's grace.

How do Galatians 5:13-14 and Mark 10:42-45 challenge you to love more like Jesus?

DAY 4
THE SHARING OF LIFE

Name the three people who have the most access to your life.

Mark an X on the continuum below to show how comfortable you are opening yourself up in vulnerability with those three people. Then, draw a circle on the continuum to show how comfortable you'd be sharing your life in that way with someone else.

uncomfortable   comfortable

If the circle you drew landed on the left side of the continuum, you're not alone! It is easier to wrap our minds around the call to love God than the call to love people because loving people involves being vulnerable. God is trustworthy; people often aren't. So in terms of human nature, Jesus's call to love like He does is revolutionary. Yet that's exactly what we see in the New Testament accounts of Christ's followers.

> *We have spoken openly to you, Corinthians; our heart has been opened wide.*
> *We are not withholding our affection from you, but you are withholding yours*
> *from us. I speak as to my children; as a proper response, open your heart to us.*
> **2 CORINTHIANS 6:11-13**

Name three adjectives to describe how Paul related to the believers in Corinth.

What did he receive in return?

How could Paul have reacted to the deficit he experienced in those relationships? How did he respond, instead?

Disciple making requires relationship. As Paul gave himself in full surrender to the Lord, he gave himself fully to other believers. In doing so, he opened himself up to the possibility of being disappointed. Yet even in the fruition of that disappointment, his expectation remained the same. We are called to share life with one another, even when that's hard to do.

Read the following verses and describe what sharing life with each other means practically.

James 5:16

Galatians 6:2

Romans 12:15

As you learn to love people like Jesus does, a shift takes place in your relationships. You begin to invite others into your world and into a relationship and fellowship with you. As you give them access to your life, you are helped to follow Jesus in full devotion, and they are, too.

Based on today's passages, what is one way you can begin sharing life with other believers more deeply in the days ahead?

DAY 5
NEXT STEPS

Hopefully, you're engaging regularly with a small group of believers. That's a great start for disciple making—if your presence there is accompanied by participation. You can sit alongside the same people in Bible study for years and never know each other's stories of coming to faith. Sometimes, we don't even know how God is moving in our lives in the present. And the reality is, if we can't share our testimony with other believers, we're not likely going to be able to share it with unbelievers.

In three to five sentences, write your story of coming to faith in Jesus Christ.

Now, use a few sentences to describe the gospel message like you might share it with an unbeliever.

Sharing the gospel and how God has worked in your life is the best way you can love people like Jesus. Will you commit to sharing your personal testimony with someone this week? Will you also partner with another believer to practice sharing the gospel message aloud? When you are able to verbalize what you know and believe, your faith takes on a whole new power!

Make two lists below. On the left, identify ways you're growing in Christ's love. On the right, identify the other ways you are seeking change, renewal, and repentance.

Growing	Changing

Do everything in love.
1 CORINTHIANS 16:14

WEEK 7

LEAD LIKE ME

START

Welcome everyone to session 7, "Lead Like Me."
Before introducing session 7, take a few minutes to review session 6.

We've been tackling some pretty tough stuff in our last few sessions. Abiding in Jesus is a beautiful invitation—right up until someone makes you mad and your human nature raises its hand. It's not easy to see people like Jesus sees them or to love people like He does. Let's not jump past what we've learned too quickly. Before we dive into our next session, let's review the last.

What are some reasons you struggle to love people like Jesus does?

What next step did you identify that God is inviting you to take?

We've seen that relationship with Jesus isn't something you do part-time. It's not half-hearted, either. Jesus's invitation is for us to come to Him in every moment with our whole selves. As we do that, we will lead others to Him.

Who is someone you consider to lead others to Jesus?
What about that person makes you see them in that way?

To prepare for video session 7, pray together.

God, help each of us accept Your invitation

to help other people grow in faith.

WATCH

Use this section to take notes as you watch video session 7.

The Great Commission lets us know how to encourage others in taking the next step in their walk with the Lord.

MATTHEW 28:18-20

We disciple others so that they can disciple others.

2 TIMOTHY 2:2

We invite people into our lives so that we can pass on what we're learning and help put their hand into the hand of Jesus.

1 CORINTHIANS 11:1

DISCUSS

After viewing the video, discuss the following questions with your group.

What did you learn from today's teaching video about what it means to lead like Jesus? What practical applications stood out to you?

Read 2 Timothy 2:2. Are there people in your life that you understand your responsibility to as Paul described to Timothy? Who are you currently inviting into your life in that way? Who can you invite into your life in that way?

What are reasons many Christians don't invite others into their lives with the kind of authenticity Jesus modeled in relationships?

What steps can we take to guard against elevating self in discipling relationships so that we only elevate Jesus?

Do you have someone in your life who disciples you? Why is it important that you always do?

Close in prayer.
Prayer Requests:

DAY 1
THE INVESTMENT
OF DISCIPLESHIP

What people and relationships reflect your commitment to discipleship?

Is it easy or hard for you to commit yourself long-term to other Christians? Why?

And let us consider one another in order to provoke love and good works, not neglecting to gather together, as some are in the habit of doing, but encouraging each other, and all the more as you see the day approaching.
HEBREWS 10:24-25

Hebrews 10:24-25 is a well-known passage often used to teach about church attendance or the importance of joining a small group. And those things are important. You can't be encouraged or encourage other people to be fully devoted to Jesus if you're never present. But discipleship is about more than mere presence. You can be present and never engage or encourage anyone.

Which of the following best sums up the message of Hebrews 10:24-25?

☐ Think about the challenges and opportunities others have to impact the world for Christ. Encourage them to boldly live the life of faith until Jesus returns.

☐ Go to church often and get involved in a small group.

We do a disservice to God's Word, ourselves, and each other when we interpret Hebrews 10:25 as, "You need to go to church." That's not the message. Discipleship is about participation as much as presence—doing life together, showing up for one another in practical ways, being with one another to communicate faith struggles and victories, and encouraging each other in faithfulness. And that takes commitment in both time and intention.

What are some actions you can take to demonstrate a commitment to other believers in the ways Hebrews 10:24-25 calls you to?

Instead, God has put the body together, giving greater honor to the less honorable, so that there would be no division in the body, but that the members would have the same concern for each other. So if one member suffers, all the members suffer with it; if one member is honored, all the members rejoice with it. Now you are the body of Christ, and individual members of it.
1 CORINTHIANS 12:24B-27

Based on these verses, how would you describe your role in the body of Christ?

If you're not there yet in relationship with other believers, how can you begin forming that kind of unified connection?

The success of your church or small group won't be measured by how many people show up any given week. Its success will be measured by how you love and encourage one another. The success of your church and small group depends on your enabling each other's success for the glory of God. The same is true of your one-on-one discipling relationships. Disciple making is a long-term commitment. You can't be faithful to Jesus without being faithful to people who follow Him.

DAY 2
THE PRIORITY
OF THE BODY

When Peter preached the gospel to the crowds of travelers gathered in Jerusalem for Passover in Acts 2, the response was incredible. Three thousand people were added to the body of Christ in one day. The early church didn't have a paid staff member over discipleship and assimilation. They didn't have a plan for next steps in place. So what happened next is truly extraordinary—and their example shows what we should prioritize as we disciple new believers today.

> *So those who accepted his message were baptized, and that day about three thousand people were added to them. They devoted themselves to the apostles' teaching, to the fellowship, to the breaking of bread, and to prayer.*
> **ACTS 2:41-42**

Is it surprising to you that baptism was the first step taken by those who had turned to Christ in faith? Why?

We should not picture the many baptisms that followed Peter's sermon as one long line of people waiting their turn to be immersed by a preacher. A more likely assumption to make is that all 3,000 who had come to faith were in the water, being baptized simultaneously.

Can you imagine the sight? The water was filled with thousands of people praising God as they came to Jesus, received His free gift of salvation, and committed to surrender their lives to Him and abide in Him for the rest of their days.

Read Romans 6:3-4. What does baptism demonstrate about a person?

Now reread Acts 2:42. What might baptism have had to do with the devotion to God and each other that came next?

Baptism is a first step of obedience that conveys a decision of commitment to Jesus and the community of faith. And as Acts 2:42 expresses, there are some other important ways we also convey that commitment.

Read the following verses and note what each teaches about the priority of commitment to following Jesus in full devotion.

Matthew 4:4

Colossians 3:16

Why must we exhort those we disciple to commit themselves to God and other believers through baptism and the study of His Word?

What problems might erupt if we continue in discipleship relationships without emphasizing those priorities?

Leading others to follow Jesus is a joy and a privilege. It is a long-term commitment, and its dynamics change over time. Our aim is not to be another person's foundation in the faith but to show them how to make Christ their foundation. When we encourage others to demonstrate their faith through baptism, get plugged into the church, and start reading God's Word, they begin to take ownership of their faith—and their commitment leads them to disciple others!

DAY 3
THE GIFT OF GOD'S WORD

What is a book you have read that you then recommended to others?

Humor, relatable illustrations, motivation, fresh insights, and self-help are typically the makings of today's best-sellers. For the most part, we like helpful tips for self-improvement and authors who leave us feeling good. We like an easy read, and we like to share those kinds of books with others—and the Bible isn't like that.

Record what the following verses express about God's Word.

Hebrews 4:12

Jeremiah 23:29

Psalm 119:105

The images God's Word uses to describe itself can make us uncomfortable. It is sharper than a sword and pierces us in the deepest places of our thoughts and hearts. It lays us naked and exposed before God, who holds us accountable for what He finds. It's also like a mirror, a hammer, and a lamp. It shows us who we are and where we need to make changes.

Why, then, is leading others learn to treasure, study, and obey God's Word the most loving thing you can do for them?

Sanctify them by the truth; your word is truth.
JOHN 17:17

*So faith comes from what is heard, and what is heard
comes through the message about Christ.*
ROMANS 10:17

Think about how you first came to faith in Jesus. Someone told you about Him, right? That person may have used a verse like Romans 6:23 so you could better understand your sin problem and how eternal life is a free gift from God through His Son, Jesus. Or they may have used some other method to share the gospel with you. Even if no one spoke to you about Jesus, you "heard" about Him through the pages of Scripture. Faith requires hearing, and hearing comes from God's Word.

In your interactions with others, are you regularly helping them learn to treasure, study, and obey God's Word? Does this happen only in scheduled Bible study groups, or does it also happen in daily life? Why?

Why does God's Word grow a person's faith far more than any life experience or earthly relationship?

Discipling others involves teaching them to obey the Word of God. The Bible leads people to become who God created them to be. His Word intends to complete the process He started when He called them to come and receive His salvation. Discipleship is not a simple or easy process, but, in love, God's Word gives all of us the truth we need to confront our issues and grow in godliness.

*All Scripture is inspired by God and is profitable for teaching, for
rebuking, for correcting, for training in righteousness, so that the
man of God may be complete, equipped for every good work.*
2 TIMOTHY 3:16-17

DAY 4
THE GRACE IN WEAKNESS

*Humble yourselves, therefore, under the mighty hand of God, so that he
may exalt you at the proper time, casting all your cares on him, because
he cares about you. Be sober-minded, be alert. Your adversary the devil
is prowling around like a roaring lion, looking for anyone he can devour.
Resist him, firm in the faith, knowing that the same kind of sufferings are
being experienced by your fellow believers throughout the world.
The God of all grace, who called you to his eternal glory in Christ, will himself restore,
establish, strengthen, and support you after you have suffered a little while.*
1 PETER 5:6-10

**Based on this passage, what should we know about each other as we engage in
discipling relationships?**

**Think of a time in your life when you grew closer to God through failure.
What factors led to that growth?**

**How do you typically respond when another believer is caught up in sin?
What role do you have in that person's restoration and growth?**

This side of heaven, failure is a part of life. Even the most well-intentioned believers
possess a nature marked by human weakness and proclivity to sin. So as you
engage in the privilege and responsibility of making disciples, it's important to
understand the people in whom you invest will struggle at times to live out the call
of full devotion—just as you yourself have struggled.

Brothers and sisters, if someone is overtaken in any wrongdoing, you
who are spiritual, restore such a person with a gentle spirit, watching out
for yourselves so that you also won't be tempted. Carry one another's
burdens; in this way you will fulfill the law of Christ. For if anyone considers
himself to be something when he is nothing, he deceives himself.
GALATIANS 6:1-3

What practical instructions are we given for how to respond when another believer sins?

Even in light of our own struggles with sin, we are often tempted to give up on others who fail to live according to God's commands. Why do we sometimes overlook or struggle with proper, biblical restoration?

Compare 1 Peter 5:6-10 to Galatians 6:1-3. What posture do these passages teach you to have as you interact with other believers?

The world does not teach the same message we find in Galatians. God not only wants us to show grace in other people's weaknesses but to help shoulder those burdens as well. Sin is a weight that holds us in bondage, and God's Word tells us to look for those around us who are struggling under that weighty bondage and help carry their load—by showing grace and restoring them in the love and humility of Christ.

Who has God placed in your life that you need to lovingly restore to faith? How will you go about doing that?

DAY 5
NEXT STEPS

Being fully devoted to Jesus involves long-term commitment—to Him and to His followers. This week, you've considered some practical ways that commitment demonstrates itself. Take a few minutes to reflect on ways you can lead others, becoming fully devoted disciples together.

SHARE YOUR LIFE WITH OTHERS.
Two are better than one because they have a good reward for their efforts.
ECCLESIASTES 4:9

ENCOURAGE OTHERS TO BE BAPTIZED AND STUDY GOD'S WORD.
Therefore we were buried with him by baptism into death,
in order that, just as Christ was raised from the dead by the
glory of the Father, so we too may walk in newness of life.
ROMANS 6:4

TEACH OTHERS TO ABIDE IN CHRIST AND OBEY HIS WORD.
I am the vine; you are the branches. The one who remains in me and
I in him produces much fruit, because you can do nothing without me.
JOHN 15:5

SHOW GRACE TO OTHERS AND RESTORE THEM WHEN THEY FAIL.
Carry one another's burdens; in this way you will fulfill the law of Christ.
GALATIANS 6:2

Record some next steps you'll take to answer Jesus's call to lead like Him.

On the left, identify ways you're growing in the personal investment of discipleship. On the right, identify the other ways you are seeking change, renewal, and repentance.

Growing	Changing

WEEK 8

SEND LIKE ME

START

Welcome everyone to session 8, "Send Like Me."
Before introducing session 8, take a few minutes to review session 7.

You've made it to the final week of our study, but the joy of being fully devoted to Jesus doesn't ever have to end. Let's finish our study strong by inviting God to replicate in others the full devotion He continues to develop in us. But, first, let's talk about what God has most recently taught us.

How have you grown in your understanding of what it means to lead like Jesus?

What next step did you identify that God is inviting you to take?

Jesus invited others into His life. As He did, discipleship occurred. And the result of those discipling relationships continues to make a difference even today! Now, we will begin to discover the most incredible reality of our entire study—God will use us to teach others to be fully devoted to Jesus.

Name one spiritual truth you most want to pass on to other people.

To prepare for video session 8, pray together.

God, help each of us accept Your invitation to let You replicate

in others the discipleship that takes place in our lives.

WATCH

Use this section to take notes as you watch video session 8.

In the Great Commission, Jesus invites us to be "all in" with Him—always and all the time.

MATTHEW 28:18-20

Jesus's devotion to His disciples was long-term, and we need to have that mentality as well.

Discipleship is helping someone else grow in their walk with the Lord and then encouraging them to help others in the same way.

DISCUSS

After viewing the video, discuss the following questions with your group.

What is something you've taught someone else to do that made you proud when you saw it play out in real life?

What have you learned in these eight weeks of study that God wants to see play out in your life? Who is someone you hope observes the changes in you that are taking place?

Read Matthew 28:18-20. How many times do you see the word "all"?
Can you be fully devoted to Jesus without investing in others to the point of sending them out as disciple makers?

Who is someone you want to send out as a disciple maker? How can God use you to make that happen?

Close in prayer.

Prayer Requests:

DAY 1
THE MULTIPLICATION
OF DEVOTION

As you've considered what it looks like to be sent out in Christ to make disciples these last few weeks—loving people like He does and committing to them in ongoing relationship—it might seem overwhelming. Maybe even impossible. After all, you know yourself and the ways you sometimes struggle to live with full devotion to Jesus. You know the challenges that come in earthly relationships, too. How in the world are you going to help others become fully devoted followers of Jesus?

In Ephesians 3, Paul prayed a prayer for believers in Ephesus that answers that very question. As he prayed that God would strengthen them with power through His Spirit, dwell in their hearts through faith, ground them in His incomprehensible love, and fill them with all His fullness, Paul reminded himself—and us—how such an enormous hope can possibly become reality.

> *Now to him who is able to do above and beyond all that we ask or think*
> *according to the power that works in us—to him be glory in the church*
> *and in Christ Jesus to all generations, forever and ever. Amen.*
> **EPHESIANS 3:20-21**

How is your full devotion to Jesus possible? How is it possible that you can disciple others to follow Jesus in full devotion?

What is the greatest outcome you can imagine taking place through your personal investment of discipleship?

God can do more. In Him, nothing is impossible (see Matthew 17:20, 19:26). You might think God can work through you to help one or two people devote themselves more fully to Jesus. Scripture assures us of a far greater outcome—

His kingdom expands through multiplication, not addition. As you invest in the spiritual growth of others, He will multiply your faithfulness.

> Read Matthew 25:14-30. Personalize this parable. Thinking specifically about the call to go and make disciples, what "talents" has God entrusted to you (e.g., relationships, positions, gifts, abilities)?

> What does the master's response indicate about God's desire for you as you await the return of Christ?

What's most important is not the amount you have been given but what you do with it. The first two servants each doubled the resources given to them by the master. They both took what they had and put it to work, unsure of the return on investment. Putting their talents to work was a risk. Yet they were faithful in the opportunity they had been given, their efforts were multiplied, and they shared in their master's joy.

> In terms of the calling that you have received to go and make disciples, which servant are you most like right now: the ones who were faithful even though risks were involved or the servant who played it safe?

> What are some practical steps you can take in faith so that God can multiply your efforts?

You have been given the opportunity to disciple others as you are being discipled. As you are sent out in Jesus each day, loving like Him in long-term commitment, God wants you to encourage and challenge others to obey Jesus and make more disciples. As you help them, they can go help others.

> *"His master said to him, 'Well done, good and faithful servant! You were faithful over a few things; I will put you in charge of many things. Share your master's joy.'"*
> **MATTHEW 25:23**

DAY 2
THE INVESTMENT
IN SENDING

Have you ever found yourself in too deep, too fast in a new endeavor? What happened?

Imagine a friend takes you up the lift to their favorite ski trail because they assume your athleticism will automatically translate into success the first day you ever hit the slopes. Your new employer inserts you into leadership on a team project already in process—without getting you up to speed on existing dynamics. It's rough! When we're put in a situation requiring knowledge and experience disproportionate to the knowledge and experience we actually have, problems arise.

Have you witnessed a situation in which someone assumed a person's readiness and they got in over their heads too deep, too fast? What problems might we face if we quickly put new disciples in leadership positions or send them out to make disciples without first showing them what discipleship looks like?

It's true that every believer in Christ is called to live as one sent on gospel mission. It's also true that every believer in Christ is meant to exist in a place of unity with other believers as they live out that calling.

Circle each action below that would indicate a person is unified with another person in making disciples. Draw a line through each action that would indicate separation and disharmony, instead.

spending time together   partnering in disciple making   teaching

inattention   encouraging   prayerlessness   helping

praying   giving correction when needed   hasty commissioning

The better tact of a friend on the slopes would be to spend time with you in ski instruction at the base of the mountain. A new employer would do well to allow you opportunity to observe the already-working team in progress before inserting you as leader. Similarly, believers should not expect new Christians to carry out the work of making disciples without unifying with them in helpful ways. Consider the example of Jesus in the verses below.

> *After this, Jesus and his disciples went to the Judean countryside,*
> *where he spent time with them and baptized.*
> **JOHN 3:22**

> *Jesus went up the mountain and summoned those he wanted, and they came*
> *to him. He appointed twelve, whom he also named apostles, to be with him,*
> *to send them out to preach, and to have authority to drive out demons.*
> **MARK 3:13-15**

Underline the phrase in each Scripture above that indicates Jesus's personal investment in sending His disciples.

Jesus's earthly ministry was short, and there were many needs to meet. Why did He prioritize spending time with His disciples?

Based on these verses, what would Jesus's disciples have seen and learned as He spent time with them?

Jesus spent time with His disciples. He called them to be with Him as He went about fulfilling His kingdom mission on earth. His example shows us that first, you make disciples together—modeling the discipleship process for them. Then, you send them out to make disciples on their own.

DAY 3
THE SEQUENCE
OF DISCIPLESHIP

Imitate me, as I also imitate Christ.
1 CORINTHIANS 11:1

How does Paul's instruction to the believers in Corinth strike you?
Circle all that apply:

arrogant	principled	idealistic	loving
purposeful	a sign of unity	wise	judgmental
valuable	domineering	relatable	unrelatable

As a stand-alone sentence at the beginning of 1 Corinthians 11, Paul's statement might seem like hubris. It's helpful, then, to know that when he wrote this letter to the church at Corinth, he did not separate his Spirit-led thoughts by chapter and verse like they are separated in our Bibles today. When we read the sentences that precede "Imitate me, as I also imitate Christ," we better understand Paul's heart and meaning.

> Read 1 Corinthians 10:31-33. What, specifically, had Jesus done that Paul imitated and wanted other believers to do?

Paul learned how to relate to other people from the example of Jesus. That example was one of self-sacrifice. In other words, Paul wasn't as concerned about his own preferences as he was about helping other people know and follow Jesus. The Corinthian believers could confirm it. Paul had lived in such a way that others could see his top priority was lifting up the name of Jesus, not making a name for himself.

What do you think other people would say is your top priority?
Why does it matter how others would answer that question?

What needs to change in your life so that others could imitate you
and grow as disciples of Jesus Christ?

Disciples who make disciples are imitable. Their example teaches others not how to get noticed for the sake of notoriety or climb the ladder of influence among Christians but to "do everything for the glory of God" (1 Corinthians 10:31). The flow of that type of discipling relationship takes place like this: I do, you watch; I do, you help; you do, I help; you do, I watch.

Consider each phrase as it relates to you as a disciple maker.

I do, you watch. Who is watching you live out your faith?

I do, you help. Name a few ways the people watching you can engage with you as you live out your faith.

You do, I help. Name a few ways you can engage with others as they live out their faith.

You do, I watch. Why is it important that you continue to notice and encourage others as they live out their faith?

Discipleship takes place organically and it also takes place with intentionality. As you live by the example of Christ, others will see that example and recognize it as worthy of imitation. As you see others living out the example of Christ you have demonstrated to them, they will be emboldened by your continued help and encouragement.

DAY 4
THE SCOPE OF DISCIPLESHIP

Have you ever seen a bow hunter positioned, poised, and ready to shoot an arrow? If so, you recognized that person's purpose, right? Who would wake up early, dress in camouflage, and sit in a tree for hours to send out an arrow with no specific purpose? No one! Neither does God let fly aimless arrows. When Jesus said, "I . . . send you" (John 20:21), He had a particular target in mind and a specific mission to accomplish.

Based on what you've learned in these eight weeks of study, summarize that target and mission God intends to accomplish in, through, and around you.

> *Jesus came near and said to them, "All authority has been given to me in heaven and on earth. Go, therefore, and make disciples of all nations, baptizing them in the name of the Father and of the Son and of the Holy Spirit, teaching them to observe everything I have commanded you. And remember, I am with you always, to the end of the age."*
> **MATTHEW 28:18-20**

Jesus gave specific instructions to His disciples. In the chart below, identify what to do, how to do it, where to do it, and the promise Jesus gave for those who carry out His Great Commission.

What	How	Where	Promise

How does the authority of Jesus affect the way you receive His commission to go and make disciples?

We can reach the world through discipleship! While that may seem like an insurmountable task, Jesus reminds us that we do not go and make disciples in our own strength or power. He goes with us, and He will be with us always—in the fullness of grace and truth and ultimate authority.

How do you sometimes complicate the simple instructions Jesus gave?

In what ways does knowing the promise of Jesus's presence make a difference in how you live out the Great Commission today?

What connection is there between Jesus's intention for discipleship and your full devotion to Him?

The mission of the church and every individual believer is to take part in Jesus's global plan to save people of every tribe, tongue, and nation. The earthly outcome of full devotion to Jesus is circular: As we grow as disciples, we understand that we are sent out in Jesus to love, commit to, and send others like Jesus. And the multiplication of Christ's commission continues with clear purpose in view—that God would be worshiped and glorified forever.

After this I looked, and there was a vast multitude from every nation, tribe, people, and language, which no one could number, standing before the throne and before the Lamb. They were clothed in white robes with palm branches in their hands. And they cried out in a loud voice:

Salvation belongs to our God, who is seated on the throne, and to the Lamb!
REVELATION 7:9-10

DAY 5
NEXT STEPS

You've come to the final Next Steps pages in this study book, but in reality, next steps for those who are fully devoted to Jesus will know no earthly end. Today's next steps, then, are designed to help you identify what God is leading you to do now and also to serve as questions you can consider again and again and again as you go forward with Jesus in faith.

What is God calling you to do?

Think about your current life context and prayerfully answer the following questions:

What situation or relationship in your life do you need to entrust to Jesus?

What sin are you wrestling with? What is Jesus inviting you to receive in Him? How can you receive it?

What thoughts, relationships, or situations do you need to surrender to Jesus? What will it cost you to do that?

How can you abide in Jesus as you surrender to Him in those areas?

In what life contexts are you living as one who has been sent out? In what contexts do you need to begin living as one who has been sent out?

What person or group of people are you struggling to love as Jesus loves? What can you do to serve and share life with them better?

In what ways are you demonstrating long-term commitment to the body of Christ?

Are you making disciples who are sent out to make other disciples? Who? How can you encourage them to stay faithful to their call to make disciples?

Don't stop pursuing Jesus. Don't stop making disciples. Don't stop encouraging other believers to step into the joy of walking with the Lord and living for Him. He is inviting you to come to Him to have abundant life, and He is sending you to share that life with others—and He is faithful to give fullness of life to those who are fully devoted to Him.

A thief comes only to steal and kill and destroy. I have come
so that they may have life and have it in abundance.
JOHN 10:10

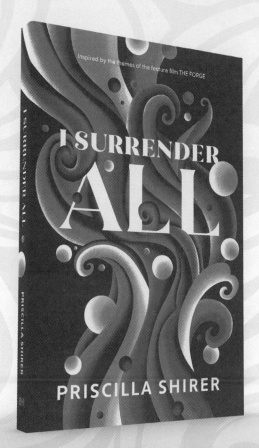

WHAT DO
YOU ALLOW
TO DEFINE
YOU?

FROM THE CREATORS OF WAR ROOM

OVERCOMER

This five-session small group Bible study uses clips from the film
OVERCOMER to examine how we determine our identity
and how we can find our true identity in Christ.

Learn more about this Bible study at lifeway.com/overcomerbiblestudy and
more about the *OVERCOMER* movie and products at lifeway.com/overcomer.

Lifeway

ALSO AVAILABLE
from the makers of

THE FORGE

In Theaters August 23, 2024

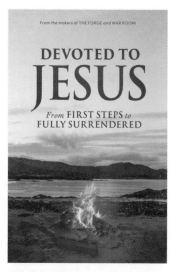

Devoted to Jesus is not only a complete guide to walking with Christ personally but also a shareable resource for helping lead others into a life of discipleship.

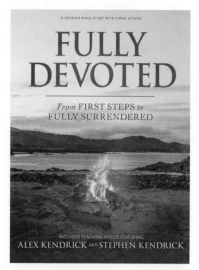

This powerful, eight-session study will take you on a journey through Jesus's invitation to follow Him and make disciples of others.

By walking through the Gospel of Luke, *Count Me In* inspires students to hear Jesus's call of discipleship and to boldly live out their faith every day.

This five-session study based on *The Forge* includes clips from the movie and will help you learn to devote yourself to Jesus and follow Him through lifelong discipleship.

Count the cost.

We must not fear what following Christ might cost us in this life, but what we are missing by withholding anything at all from Him.

In a culture of rampant confusion and half-hearted beliefs, people desperately need to see followers of Jesus living sincerely and wholeheartedly for Him. It's time to show this generation what it means to be fully devoted. This study will help you:

- Gain a biblical understanding of the gospel and the call of discipleship

- Place deepening trust in Jesus and give your all to Him

- Teach and serve others in the manner that Jesus would

- Encourage others to become true disciples

To enrich your study experience, be sure to access the videos available through a redemption code printed in this *Bible Study Book*.

ADDITIONAL RESOURCES

***Fully Devoted* eBOOK**
Includes the content of this printed book but offers the convenience and flexibility that come with mobile technology.

Bible Study eBook with Video Access

005849654 **$19.99**

More resources can be found online at lifeway.com/theforge

Price and availability subject to change without notice.